God's Plan for Humanity
Volume 1

Tribulation and Deliverance

James Malm

ISBN 978-1-7753510-2-3

Copyright © 2015 James David Malm
All Rights Reserved

Unless otherwise noted all scripture quotes are taken
from the King James Version of the Bible

Dedication

This work is dedicated to the Great God whose house is eternity; the Father and Sovereign of all that exists and the sum of all Truth, Wisdom, Love, Justice and Mercy.
May God's house be filled with children whose chief joy is to be like Him!

Visit Our Website
theshininglight.info

Table of Contents

God's Plan for Humanity 7
    The Plan of God 8
    Why Suffering? 11

The Next Few Years 15
    The World Today 16
    The Final Signs Before the Great Tribulation 19
    The Great Tribulation Begins with the Fall of Jerusalem and Judea 22
    The Fall of the Anglo Saxon People 27
    The New Europe Attacks Asia 36
    The Armies of Asia Attack Jerusalem 38
    The Coming of Messiah the Christ 41

The Millennium 49
    Pentecost: God's Spirit Poured Out On All Flesh 50
    The Millennial Kingdom of God 57
    The End of Satan 67
    Daniel 2: Babylon the Great Totally Destroyed 72
    The Restoration of Israel 82
    Germany, Austro-Hungary [Assyria] 93
    Egypt 103
    Turkey 105

Key Prophecies 113
    Daniel 8: The 2300 Days 114
    Ezekiel 4 126
    Dating the Coming of Messiah 131
    Daniel 9: The 70 Weeks Prophecy 133

Appendix 1 145
    Biblical Nations Identified 146
    The Descendants of Japheth 148
    The Descendants of Ham 150
    The Descendants of Shem 154
    Ammon and Moab: Modern Jordan 159

- The Arab Peoples 161
- The Hagarenes 163
- Esau 164

Appendix 2 167
- The Family of Abraham 168
- Modern Locations of the Twelve Tribes of Israel 174
- Possession of the Promised Land 184

God's Plan for Humanity

The Plan of God

Man is born, lives a short space and dies with generation after generation perishing like the flowers which blooms and is gone. The transitory nature of the flesh has prompted people to ask the question "Is this all there is?" from time immemorial.

This book is the beginning of a five volume series on "God's Plan for Humanity" which will answer that question and explain God's purpose in creating mankind.

No, this is NOT all there is; and yes God had a purpose in creating humanity as temporary transitory flesh! In reality the physical human being is only part of a process of creating something much more lasting!

The flesh was never intended to be permanent; it is part of a process of creating something eternal! Human beings were created flesh so that they could learn those behavior patterns which would allow mankind to live in peace and prosperity as realize the need for something better. How?

Just look at all of the violence and problems that human beings have brought upon themselves in this world. What if man had been created eternal and indestructible, consider how much worse those problems would be.

God made us flesh so that we could learn through experience that we need to listen to and obey God our Father to achieve a lasting and successful society where no person oppresses any other person.

All successful societies have rules which govern the behavior of their citizens, protect people from one another and maintain the peace in order that all might prosper. To have universal peace and prosperity there must be universal laws respected and obeyed by all people everywhere.

Therein lies the problem: Every person or group of persons has a different set of behavioral rules and each one thinks that their ways are best. At the same time each person and groups of persons [families or nations, religions etc] is proud of their own ways and behaves selfishly trying to dominate others. That is the cause of strife between people and wars between nations: Every one wants to get their own way!

God made us transitory flesh so that we could try our own ways out and learn from experience; that only God the Father has the experience, wisdom and love for ALL people to make laws which will gender peace and prosperity for ALL people.

Today every people and nation follows their own ways and clashes with others; that simple will not work! It will not bring peace to the earth!

Humanity needs an ultimate moral authority of such experience, wisdom and love that all human beings will respect and obey that authority; and that authority must also have the power to put down any potential rebellion.

Mankind was created flesh so that humanity could learn through experience that they cannot achieve peace on their own. Only then will ALL people accept a Higher Moral Authority!

The plan of God for humanity begins by making us physical and allowing us to make our mistakes without overmuch divine intervention so that we can learn to respect, love and obey God our Father and to live by every Word of God.

Once we learn that our own ways bring suffering decay and death, and that God's ways protect all people bringing peace and prosperity, we are ready for the second phase which is sincere repentance from doing as we please and a commitment to live by every Word of God in future.

This will be covered in detail in Volume 2 "Personal Salvation."

We must then go through a period of learning the Word of God and applying those ways in our own lives.

Volume 3 explains the functions of the priesthood/ministry and limits and parameters of ecclesiastical authority.

Volume's 4 ad 5 cover the Biblical Festivals which explain that a small number of people are called to God at this time, so that they could come to God while observing the situation in the world today; and that ALL of humanity who have ever lived and died will resurrected back to flesh and will then be given their opportunity to turn to God and learn the way ot eternal life as well.

Ultimately God will change to eternal spirit all those who in their proper time have had the opportunity to come to God and who have internalized the nature of God through learning and living by every Word of God.

Why Suffering?

The scriptures tell us that a Time of Great Trouble will come upon this world which will bring the coming of Messiah the Christ to deliver humanity and usher in a millennial Sabbath of rest and peace for humanity.

There is a great hope for humanity, yet for recorded history humanity has rejected that hope and must first be humbled until they are willing to accept the wisdom of God.

The Creator had lived for untold eternities and we men live for a hundred years maybe. Yet the vast majority of humanity has not followed the word and wisdom of God through all of recorded history.

Man follows his own ways which means disaster since many men follow different ways contrary to one another and man lacks the billions of years of experience and the wisdom of God.

Since creation man has lived in rebellion against the wisdom of God; living by his own ways.

Oh, yes, many claim to follow God, but do they really live by every Word of God, or are they just using God to exalt themselves and their own ways? How many bloody wars have been fought with all sides claiming that God is on their side?

Man must be humbled and his great pride broken before he will accept the coming of Messiah as King of all kings and bow to the will of God.

At creation man was given a choice to obey God or to decide for himself what is right and what is wrong and man chose to reject the wisdom of God and to decide for himself.

When he made the man, God planted a wondrous garden for him; which was an allegory of the paradise that man could have if he only obeyed God. Revelation 22 is the real thing that the physical Garden in Eden was meant to picture.

Genesis 2:8 And the LORD God planted a garden eastward in Eden; and there he put the man whom he had formed. **2:9** And out of the ground made the LORD God to grow every tree that is pleasant to the sight, and good for food; the tree of life also in the midst of the garden, and

The man was placed in Eden and told to care for it. Thus the lordship of man was coupled with responsibility to care for that which was placed under his control.

Genesis 2:15 And the LORD God took the man, and put him into the garden of Eden to dress it and to keep it.

At this point God gives the man and woman a choice and forces a decision by allowing them to be tempted.

The tree of the knowledge of good and evil, represented deciding for ourselves what is right and wrong, instead of standing on and obeying the whole word of God.

This tree may have been any tree and its fruit physically may well have been good; but the command not to eat of this tree was a TEST to see if the man would obey God in all things, or if they would follow their own desires to do what they decided for themselves.

2:16 And the LORD God commanded the man, saying, Of every tree of the garden thou mayest freely eat: **2:17** But of the tree of the knowledge of good and evil, thou shalt not eat of it: for in the day that thou eatest thereof thou shalt surely die.

Genesis 3

Satan in physical form looked like a flying serpent which we Anglo Saxons call a dragon. The Aztecs, Toltec's and Maya worship the flying serpent, calling it Quetzalcoatl; and sacrificed thousands to Satan in this form, while others did the same sacrificing vast numbers of human beings while worshiping Satan as the sun god or as the flying serpent or dragon.

The term translated "serpent" is from the word "hiss" H 5172, here meant to be the flying serpent dragon / dragon Satan. Satan being referred to as a dragon [flying serpent] in Rev 12:3-17, Rev 13:2 and 13:4, Rev 16:13 and Rev 20:2.

Satan begins to entice the woman by bringing up the subject of the forbidden fruit.

Now very carefully here: God did not say that the fruit would kill; he said that the act of eating the fruit would kill; for the wages of sin [living contrary to the way that brings life] is death. The nature of this fruit had nothing to do with the issue, which issue is: Will we zealously keep the whole word of God or will we decide right and wrong for ourselves?

Whether it is eating a fruit that God forbade to eat, or idolizing the words of men above the word of God, to follow men and turn away from any zeal for the word of God: Any departure, watering down, or compromising with any part of the whole word of God, is deciding for ourselves to do what we want, instead of following the wisdom of God.

The woman and then the man lost their zeal for keeping and obeying the word of God. They decided right and wrong for themselves by taking the forbidden fruit, instead of obeying the word of God!

Genesis 3:1 Now the serpent was more subtil than any beast of the field which the LORD God had made. And he said unto the woman, Yea, hath God said, Ye shall not eat of every tree of the garden? **3:2** And the woman said unto the serpent, We may eat of the fruit of the trees of the garden: **3:3** But of the fruit of the tree which is in the midst of the garden, God hath said, Ye shall not eat of it, neither shall ye touch it, lest ye die.

Satan told the woman that she would not die if she rejected the word of God to decide right and wrong for herself!

This is the same lie being told to the brethren by Satan through most of their religious leaders today! They say in so many words: "God doesn't mind if we are lax for his Word and zealous for our own ways! We are

God's people and whatever we do, must be right, because God left us in charge. Obey us and do not question us by God's word, for we are leaders in place of, or between God and the brethren."

Then Satan told the big lie saying that they would not die or suffer if they rejected the wisdom of God to decide for themselves; but that lie was couched in the context of the fruit and the woman and most of humanity since then has always looked on this as a decision about eating fruit; and has missed the point that the real issue was about living by every Word of God, or deciding right and wrong for ourselves.

3:4 And the serpent said unto the woman, Ye shall not surely die: **3:5** For God doth know that in the day ye eat thereof, then your eyes shall be opened, and ye shall be as gods, knowing good and evil.

Deciding for ourselves always looks good to those who have no love for the Word of God. We love self more than we love God, and because of this self love and self exaltation and pride; we are led away from any zeal for the whole word of God as Eve was.

3:6 And when the woman saw that the tree was good for food, and that it was pleasant to the eyes, and a tree to be desired to make one wise, she took of the fruit thereof, and did eat, and gave also unto her husband with her; and he did eat.

From that day forward until today the vast majority of humanity has been eating the forbidden fruit by doing what they want, doing what they think is right; and not living by the word of God.

The Next Few Years

The World Today

The Scriptures tell us that an "hour of trial" is coming on all the earth to humble humanity and to make us ready to accept the coming of Messiah to save us.

The scriptures tell us that this "hour of trial" or great tribulation will begin in a time of peace.

Daniel 8:23 And in the latter time of their kingdom, when the transgressors are come to the full, a king of fierce countenance, and understanding dark sentences, shall stand up.

8:24 And his power shall be mighty, but not by his own power: and he shall destroy wonderfully, and shall prosper, and practise, and shall destroy the mighty and the holy people.

8:25 And through his policy also he shall cause craft to prosper in his hand; and he shall magnify himself in his heart, and **by [in] peace shall destroy many**: he shall also stand up against the Prince of princes; but he shall be broken without hand.

1 Thessalonians 5:1 But of the times and the seasons, brethren, ye have no need that I write unto you.

5:2 For yourselves know perfectly that the day of the Lord so cometh as a thief in the night.

5:3 For when they shall say, Peace and safety; then sudden destruction cometh upon them, as travail upon a woman with child; and they shall not escape.

This tells us that a peace deal will come in the Middle East

In order for a regional peace deal the Islamic State and other Islamic Extremists must be and will be defeated in the Middle East!

After that Hamas and Hezbollah will have to be dealt with and new peace oriented governments in Israel, Palestine, Gaza, Syria and Iran will be needed to set the conditions for a genuine peace deal.

That presupposes a major regional conflict, with Israel defeating the Hamas Military Wing, and war spreading to defeat Hezbollah and quite likely changing the regimes in Syria and Iran.

Such a regional conflict could well bring the West and Russia to the point of serious confrontation; and any blockage of the Persian Gulf shipping lanes could trigger world financial difficulties.

Watch for:

1. The defeat of organized Islamic Extremism in Syria / Iraq

2. A change of regime in Syria

3. Another Gaza conflict resulting in severe defeat for the Hamas Military Wing and related organizations

4. The Gaza conflict escalating in a multi front war including Hezbollah, ending with the defeat of Hezbollah

5. The possibility of a takedown of the Revolutionary Guard and a regime change in Iran

6. A possible confrontation between Russia and the West; with potential repercussions for Ukraine and Europe

7. A potential international financial crisis

8. The establishment of peace oriented governments in Israel and the Middle East

9. A British exit from the EU resulting in other nations following suite and bringing an EU crisis

10. A genuine regional dialogue for peace and the signing and ratifying of a peace agreement, including Gaza and Palestine

11. A deployment of peacekeepers

12. Either the present pope or a new pope in the Vatican, being empowered to do miracles

13. The miracle working pope almost immediately calling for a New Federal Europe and through his influence bringing it to life in a matter of weeks

14. Ten nations responding and giving their military and external affairs over to a common leader to form a New Federal Europe system.

The Final Signs Before the Great Tribulation

1. The empowering of a pope to do miracles

> **Revelation 13:13** And he doeth great wonders, so that he maketh fire come down from heaven on the earth in the sight of men,
>
> **13:14** And deceiveth them that dwell on the earth by the means of those miracles which he had power to do in the sight of the beast; saying to them that dwell on the earth, that they should make an image [likeness] to the beast [of the Holy Roman Empire church state federal system], which had the wound by a sword [Mussolini's Concordat with the Vatican], and did live.

This miracle worker will use his influence to bring the dead Babylonian Holy Roman Empire church state system back to life.

2. The rise of a New Federal Europe at the instigation of the miracle working pope, to which ten nations will give their power.

> **Revelation 17:12** And the ten horns which thou sawest are ten kings, which have received no kingdom as yet; but receive power as kings one hour with the beast.
>
> **17:13 These have one mind, and shall give their power and strength unto the beast.**

3. After the present Mideast wars, a peace deal being agreed and ratified; and Peace and Safety being declared

> **1 Thessalonians 5:3** For when they shall say, Peace and safety; then sudden destruction cometh upon them, as travail upon a woman with child; and they shall not escape.

4. The city of Jerusalem and the Jewish State being surrounded by peacekeepers

> **Luke 21:20** And **when ye shall see Jerusalem compassed with armies, then know that the desolation thereof is nigh.**
>
> **21:21** Then let them which are in Judaea flee to the mountains; and let them which are in the midst of it depart out; and let not them that are in the countries enter thereinto.
>
> **21:22** For these be the days of vengeance, that all things which are written may be fulfilled.

5. The miracle working religious leader will visits Jerusalem and go to the Holy Mount approximately 75 days after he is given power to do miracles; and the great tribulation will begin immediately

> **Matthew 24:15 When ye therefore shall see the abomination of desolation, spoken of by Daniel the prophet, stand in the holy place,** (whoso readeth, let him understand:)
>
> **24:16** Then let them which be in Judaea flee into the mountains:
>
> **24:17** Let him which is on the housetop not come down to take any thing out of his house:

24:18 Neither let him which is in the field return back to take his clothes.

24:19 And woe unto them that are with child, and to them that give suck in those days!

24:20 But pray ye that your flight be not in the winter, neither on the sabbath day:

24:21 For then shall be great tribulation, such as was not since the beginning of the world to this time, no, nor ever shall be.

The Great Tribulation Begins with the Fall of Jerusalem and Judea

After the present wars destroy Islamic Extremism in the Middle East and reset regional realities, a genuine dialogue for peace will come and a peace deal will be reached, ratified, and begin to be implemented with the deployment of peacekeepers to enforce the deal.

A miracle working pope will be set up in the Vatican and will call for Europe's nations to give their security, foreign affairs and military to a single leader in a New Federal European system. This system has already been planned out and is supported by the Vatican and the Catholic [Christian democratic] political parties in Europe; therefore it will rise suddenly and very quickly.

Ten nations will join this United Europe which will be allied with and supported by many nations around the world especially the strong Catholic and Muslim [except Egypt] nations.

The peace deal will have been approved by Israel; but the minority Jewish Extremist Settler Movement will be bitterly opposed.

When Peace and Safety (1 Thess 5:3), is declared to have been achieved and the miracle working Pope goes to the Holy Place [Temple Mount] the peace deal will be sabotaged by the Jewish Settler Movement Extremist Minority (Mat 24:15). Egypt may also provoke the New Europe in some other way as well.

Then because of our overspreading sin, God will remove his protection and will allow the Palestinians and Gazan supported by the surrounding nations to rise up and rush into the Jewish State from the north and Gaza in the south as well as from the West Bank.

The world's Roman Catholic nations [which include all of Latin America and much of Europe and much people elsewhere], will support whatever this miracle worker endorses, while the Islamic nations will be outraged at the failure of the peace deal.

When the Islamic nations of Psalm 83 invade the land there will be a blood bath and Israel can be expected to prepare a nuclear holocaust for the invading nations forcing the New Europe to intervene to secure those weapons and stop the bloodshed.

Most of the world will also be outraged at the Jewish Extremists and will be supportive of the New Europe. Almost the entire world, tired of war and disgusted with the Jewish Settler Movement Extremists will applaud the move; however things will not stop there.

At some point the New Europe will enter Egypt and take control over the Suez Canal and that nation.

The whole book of Deuteronomy repeats over and over that possession of the land is absolutely CONDITIONAL on faithfully living by every Word of God.

The Psalm 83 Prophecy

Psalm 83:1 Keep not thou silence, O God: hold not thy peace, and be not still, O God.

83:2 For, lo, thine enemies make a tumult: and they that hate thee have lifted up the head.

83:3 They have taken crafty counsel against thy people, and consulted against thy hidden ones.

83:4 They have said, Come, and let us cut them off from being a nation; that the name of Israel may be no more in remembrance.

83:5 For they have consulted together with one consent: they are confederate against thee:

83:6 The tabernacles of Edom [Turkey], and the Ishmaelites [true Arabs, sons of Ishmael; sons of Abraham and Agar (Hagar)]; of Moab [northern Jordan today], and the Hagarenes [Arabs who are sons of Agar by another than Abraham, and also not the sons of Ishmael];

83:7 Geba [Lebanon], and Ammon [southern Jordan today], and Amalek [a tribe of the Turks]; the Philistines [Gaza] with the inhabitants of Tyre [Lebanon];

83:8 Assur [Germany, Austro-Hungary] also is joined with them: they have holpen the children of Lot [will help modern Jordan; Ammon and Moab].

Selah.

Jerusalem will fall and be occupied for a full 42 months.

Revelation 11:2 But the court which is without the temple leave out, and measure it not; for it is given unto the Gentiles: and **the holy city shall they tread under foot forty and two months.**

The whole book of Deuteronomy repeats over and over that possession of the land is absolutely CONDITIONAL on faithfully living by every Word of God.

The New Europe here called the king of the north, shall be provoked by Egypt / Israel, the king of the south

Judea shall fall one last time

Daniel 11:40 And at the time of the end shall the king of the south [Egypt / the Jewish State] push at him: and the king of the north [the New Europe] shall come against him like a whirlwind, with chariots, and with horsemen, and with many ships; and he shall enter into the countries, and shall overflow and pass over.

11:41 He shall enter also into the glorious land [the Promised Land], and many countries shall be overthrown: but these shall escape out of his hand, even Edom, and Moab, and the chief of the children of Ammon [who will be allied with the New Europe Psalm 83].

The tribes of Ephraim [the British people] and Manasseh [the Anglo Saxon people of America] will also fall with Judah.

Judea will be occupied, but Britain and America will suffer a cascading collapse; beginning with economic collapse after the Arab states lead the world in abandoning the Petrodollar for the Europeans.

Hosea 5:4 They will not frame their doings to turn unto their God: for the spirit of whoredoms [departure from God as a wicked wife departs from her husband] is in the midst of them, and they have not known the LORD.

5:5 And **the pride of Israel doth testify to his face: therefore shall Israel and Ephraim fall in their iniquity: Judah also shall fall with them.**

Many of those Jews not killed will be concentrated in ghettos in the land; and many will be deported as the Lebanese broker, and the Palestinians sell them to the nations for hard labour in order to take them out of the land.

Joel 3:4 Yea, and what have ye to do with me, **O Tyre, and Zidon, and all the coasts of Palestine?** will ye render me a recompence? and if ye recompense me, swiftly and speedily will I return your recompence upon your own head;

3:5 Because ye have taken my silver and my gold, and have carried into your temples my goodly pleasant things:

3:6 The children also of Judah and the children of Jerusalem have ye sold unto the Grecians, that ye might remove them far from their border.

This hour of trial will last 42 months

Daniel 7:25 And he [the leader of the New Europe] shall speak great words against the most High, and shall wear out the saints of the most High, and think to change times and laws: and they shall be given into his hand until a time [one year] and times [plus two years] and the dividing of time [one half year: For a total of 3 1/2 years or 42 months].

Daniel 12:6 And one said to the man clothed in linen, which was upon the waters of the river, How long shall it be to the end of these wonders?

12:7 And I heard the man clothed in linen, which was upon the waters of the river, when he held up his right hand and his left hand unto heaven, and sware by him that liveth for ever that it shall be for a time, times, and an half [3 1/2 years or 42 months]; **and when he shall have accomplished to scatter the power of the holy people, all these things shall be finished** [Messiah will come].

Joseph [the Anglo Saxon people] and Judah the beloved of God shall then sincerely repent and turn to wholeheartedly embrace the Eternal, and will be saved by Messiah at the end of 42 months.

The Fall of the Anglo Saxon People

There is going to be a military crisis in the world which will a strong New Federal Europe as a balance between east and west.

This has been plotted by the Judeo Anglo American establishment for decades now, and they expect to control this new entity, however God will intervene and Satan will rise up to fight God (Daniel 12, Revelation 12).

Satan will be defeated and cast back down to the earth, and the Judeo Anglo American establishment will lose control, so that the prophets will be fulfilled. This war in heaven is spiritual and we may see no sign of this on the earth, but it has been recorded for our instruction concerning the overall events, and to encourage us that God is far mightier than Satan.

When Satan is cast down, he will empower a man in the Vatican with the ability to do miracles which has been restrained until that time.

Today there are five million Muslims and seventy million Catholics in the United States alone, along with millions of Protestants and other peace lovers; who will support the Miracle Working Pope whatever their political persuasion.

This man of sin will be seen as a great man of peace and will be looked to as an ultimate moral authority by nearly all religions including Muslims, mainstream Judaism and professing Christians.

The New World Order plan will already exist at least on paper, but it will be this miracle worker and the deceptive power of Satan which will cause the nations to agree to the plan.

The New Europe will probably acquire the massive quantities of American military supplies already prepositioned in Europe, making Europe an instant superpower will seriously reducing American military strength.

This new Europe being a Catholic creation will be allied to all the Catholic nations including Latin America, and will also quickly become allied with Turkey and the Islamic nations except for Egypt which remain in the Judeo American orbit for a very short time longer until America can no longer support them.

Along with the rise of Europe there will be a general Mideast peace deal which will bring many peacekeepers into Palestine and around Jerusalem from various nations probably including a strong Muslim contingent.

When peace and safety is declared and this pope goes to the temple mount approximately 75 days after being set up, the Settlement Movement Jews will sabotage the deal.

Mainstream Judaism will approve the peace deal but the minority Settler Movement people will sabotage the peace.

The Fifth Book of Moses tells us plainly that possession of the land is entirely dependent on living by every Word of God, which neither Israel nor the Jews do today.

Please see our "Deuteronomy Joshua" book.

God tells us that because of our sins, God will give us over to severe correction.

When the peace is broken, the Palestinians and Gazans will rise up and the Turks and neighbouring nations will pour into Jerusalem and Judea, because God has given them over to severe correction.

There will be a tremendous bloodbath as Palestinians enraged after decades of mistreatment, will give out much more than they had received.

The New Europe will be forced to act in the name of peace to secure the Israeli nuclear weapons and main military sites, and the mainstream Jews might well beg Europe to stop the blood bath.

European forces will secure areas and herd Jews into ghettos for their own safety, and will begin to deport them from Palestine to other nations at the insistence of the Palestinians, Turks and Islamic nations, completely reversing the Jewish movement into Palestine of the past one hundred years.

Despite the slaughter and deportations, many Jews will still remain in Jerusalem and Judea when Messiah comes, but it is possible that most Jews will be removed from areas north of Jerusalem; which will make way for the return of the ten tribes when Christ comes.

The United States has been over spending at a furious rate for decades now and the only thing saving the dollar and the US economy is the use of the dollar as the world's international reserve currency, especially in energy transactions where it is widely known as the Petrodollar.

For the past two decades America has also sought to internationalize its economy with the goal of creating an interdependent world controlled by the Judeo Anglo American Establishment. These two things are now America's Achilles Heel.

Scripture tell us that the tribulation will begin with the occupation of Jerusalem and Judea, and while we are told that Israel, primarily the US and Britain, will fall with Judah (Hosea 5:5); nowhere do the scripture say that the US will be nuked and instantly destroyed, or even occupied.

This idea is absolutely wrong, for the scriptures do say that Israel will fall in a process over a period of 3 1/2 years.

Daniel 12:7 And I heard the man clothed in linen, which was upon the waters of the river, when he held up his right hand and his left hand unto heaven, and sware by him that liveth for ever that it shall be for a time, times, and an half [42 thirty day months]; and **when he shall have accomplished to scatter the power of the holy people, all these things shall be finished.**

Over the past few years the present world financial system has been slowly readjusted from being solely dependent on the US Dollar to a basket of currencies and Special Drawing Rights.

This may be further adjusted over time but the situation is now already set up for a departure from the dollar.

Once the New Europe is set up and then Palestine the surrounding nations rush in on a Jewish State from which God has withdrawn his protection there will be a bloodbath.

Many of the mainstream Jews might urgently call for international intervention to stop that blood bath, at the same time it would be imperative for international forces to act immediately to secure the Israeli nuclear arsenal and massive stockpiles of armaments.

European forces will move to carry out those tasks, very probably with the consent of the US and mainstream Jewry.

How will God bring America and the British people down?

Very simply!

The Muslim countries would be grateful to Europe and would agree with its ruler to abandon the US Dollar as the Petro Dollar, and to use the Euro [or any possible new European currency] for all their energy and international transactions.

The Catholic nations [I am thinking of Latin America] as well as Asian nations would quickly jump to follow suit - if they want to buy energy; and that would bring the end of the US Dollar and initiate an economic collapse with all of its attendant catastrophes on the United States, Canada, Australia, New Zealand, Britain and other dollar dependant countries.

The inability to import products upon which the US has become dependent including oil, would result in a cascading collapse of the ability to grow and distribute food, medicine and other essentials.

No more water bombing wild fires, no more emergency help in case of hurricane, tornado, earthquake or flood. Riots are coming over race and limited resources - especially food - that will make the Watts riots seem like a picnic.

Thinking of the National Petroleum Reserve?

The maximum total withdrawal capability from the SPR is only 4.4 million barrels per day (700,000 m^3/d), so the entire inventory would be exhausted in 158 days, or about five months.

If oil imports were interrupted due to a collapse of the dollar, the United States would have less than one half of its daily import needs [or only 3/4ths of its consumption needs] for only about five months.

After that, emergency oil supplies would run out and consumption would have to be reduced to the approximately 9 million bpd of domestic production, or about one half of the present rate of consumption.

This does not take into account the possibility of interruptions in domestic production which would be quite likely in a chaotic environment.

America can be brought down without a single shot being fired!

As America collapses she will no longer be able to support her client states like Egypt, Ethiopia and other African countries and they will come under the control of Europe.

The United States and Britain, full of pride in their own wisdom and power and not recognizing that God is against them and about to correct them, will face overwhelming internal upheaval and possible cyber-attacks on their military-security, financial systems.

The deep divisions between the large minorities in America and Britain must also be added to the equation.

America and the British peoples will face internal racial and religious problems and economic crisis as the world's nations abandon the US dollar bringing economic collapse to America.

God will also withhold the rain and the present droughts will seem like the good times in comparison to the coming 1,260 day tribulation.

Huge numbers will die by internal violence, starvation and disease.

Take away those welfare cheques and food stamps; cut off the flow of cocaine from the noses of people, and end the flow of heroin into the veins of millions; take the fuel out of the cars and the food out of the mouths of the masses; then see what happens.

Riots will further disrupt distribution centers and overwhelm medical facilities, which will already be overwhelmed by a population weakened with hunger and afflicted by disease epidemics. Even the escape of deliberately engineered diseases in the turmoil and then entering the population cannot be discounted.

Little fuel to plough, till, sow, cultivate, harvest, process and transport crops; and much of what is sown will be lost to drought, pests and disease, or be demanded by the victors bringing starvation to the masses.

A starving population will be afflicted by diseases such as influenza, or one of the more modern treatment resistant diseases. Mass epidemics, and depleted medical facilities will not be able to cope; hence massive deaths from disease and pestilence.

Pestilence is the crop eating insects and rodents that eat the crops in the fields and will enter the storage bins and eat up much of the stored foodstuffs while spreading disease as well.

Judah will be occupied for three and one half years while America will collapse over a period of three and one half years.

In the third year God will begin to deliver us. Europe will go to war against Asia; and at the end of three and one half years from the initial fall of Jerusalem; Messiah the Christ will come.

Amos 4:7 And also I have withholden the rain from you, when there were yet three months to the harvest: and I caused it to rain upon one city, and caused it not to rain upon another city: one piece was rained upon, and the piece whereupon it rained not withered.

Today's drought is only the very early beginning warning; soon the drought will become so severe in the tribulation [when it is possible that no rain at all will come to our peoples], so that the thirsty will be forced to migrate for lack of water.

4:8 So two or three cities wandered unto one city, to drink water; but they were not satisfied: yet have ye not returned unto me, saith the LORD.

In our days as in those days of the ancient past, the people will gather together for the available water. Today because we are full of the same sins: God is beginning to withhold the blessing of rain and dew in due season. In the tribulation there will be much thirst, famine and starvation.

4:9 I have smitten you with blasting and mildew [fungal infestations and disease of our crops]: when your gardens and your vineyards and your fig trees and your olive trees increased, [when our plants actually produce fruit pests will eat up the produce] the palmerworm devoured them: yet have ye not returned unto me, saith the LORD.

God will do these things to crush our pride in our own ways and humble us to sincere repentance before him.

Amos 5:1 Hear ye this word which I take up against you, even a lamentation, O house of Israel.

This is the correction of this latter day tribulation which is now very close at hand.

5:2 The virgin of Israel is fallen; she shall no more rise: she is forsaken upon her land; there is none to raise her up.

God here speaks of only ten percent surviving his correction, and only a small remnant of Israel/Judah will survive the wars, famine, thirst, starvation and disease that is about to come upon us.

5:3 For thus saith the Lord GOD; **The city that went out by a thousand shall leave an hundred, and that which went forth by an hundred shall leave ten**, to the house of Israel.

Therefore quickly repent, while God may be found: for our punishment for our own sins is the same. God will afflict our flesh in the hope that he may humble us and save our spirit.

5:4 For **thus saith the LORD unto the house of Israel, Seek ye me, and ye shall live:**

5:5 But seek not Bethel [Be diligently zealous to follow and to live by every Word of God and do not follow idols of men. Do not put your trust in fortifications and cities (the strength of men) of men, but put your trust in the Eternal God!], nor enter into Gilgal, and pass not to Beersheba: for Gilgal shall surely go into captivity, and Bethel shall come to nought.

5:6 Seek the LORD, and ye shall live; [Sincerely repent and be diligently zealous to live by EVERY WORD of God.] lest he break out like fire in the house of Joseph [both physical and apostate spiritual Israel], and devour it, and there be none to quench it in Bethel

Our idols of men and our false traditions will not save us.

It is WE who must seek God the Father, for if the spiritually called out will not turn to zealously live by every Word of God and our salt of passionate zeal for godliness has lost its savor; how can anyone be saved at all?

5:7 Ye who turn judgment to wormwood [we who pervert godly judgment into the bitterness of injustice], and leave [turn away from] off righteousness [godliness] in the earth,

5:8 Seek him that maketh the seven stars and Orion, and turneth the shadow of death into the morning [turns death into the bright morning of life], and maketh the day dark with night: that calleth for the waters of the sea, and poureth them out upon the face of the earth: The LORD is his name:

5:9 That strengtheneth the spoiled against the strong, so that the spoiled shall come against the fortress.

The whole world will strongly support the actions of the New Europe, who would be regarded as acting to bring peace.

The New Europe here called the king of the north; will be provoked and will occupy Judea; while America and the British nations collapse.

The New Europe with her allies will take over the Jewish State and Egypt; and with the collapse of the Anglo Americans, they will also take control of Egypt and the African and other client states of America and Britain.

Daniel 11:40 And at the time of the end shall the king of the south [Egypt / the Jewish State] push at him: and the king of the north [the New Europe] shall come against him like a whirlwind, with chariots, and with horsemen, and with many ships; and he shall enter into the countries, and shall overflow and pass over.

11:41 He shall enter also into the glorious land [the Promised Land], and many countries shall be overthrown: but these shall escape out of his hand, even Edom, and Moab, and the chief of the children of Ammon [who will be allied with the New Europe Psalm 83].

The New Europe will occupy Judah and will take control of Egypt; inheriting the African, Latin American client states of the Judeo Anglo Saxon Establishment.

Daniel 11:42 He [the New Europe] shall stretch forth his hand also upon the countries: and the land of Egypt shall not escape.

11:43 But he shall have power over the treasures of gold and of silver, and over all the precious things of Egypt: and the Libyans and the Ethiopians shall be at his steps.

It is quite possible that the US would just give the 480 B61 American nuclear weapons [180 of which are already under European control] and the huge US military equipment assets stored in Europe. If not, the New Europe could just walk in and take them over [perhaps for the US debt] when America collapses.

In addition, the capture of the massive American weapons inventory stored in Israel along with Israel's nuclear weapons would make the New Europe into an instant super power.

After the defeat of the Jewish State and the collapse of the Anglo Saxon nations, control of the American and British client states like Egypt, Ethiopia, Latin America and most of Africa, would make the New Europe an instant mega super power

> A report by the Institute for Science and International Security claims that Israel has 115 nuclear warheads and some 660 kg of plutonium.

The New Europe called by God "Babylon the Great" will become incredibly rich and prosperous over the first two years; and then in the third year she shall make a fatal mistake.

The New Europe Attacks Asia

Today America is planning for a existential conflict with Asia. The Asian nations are rising around the Shanghai Cooperation Organization.

Current Nov 2015

1. Member States: Kazakhstan. China. Kyrgyzstan. Russia. Tajikistan. Uzbekistan.
2. Observer States: Afghanistan. India. Iran. Mongolia. Pakistan.
3. Dialogue Partners: Belarus. Turkey. Sri Lanka.

While Turkey will ally with the New Europe the nations of Asia will ultimately ally together and will be seen as a threat by Europe.

This organization is a developing economic and military partnership.

The American actions in the Middle East and plans to build up in Asia, after Balkanizing the Mideast nations to control the regions resources, are a part of this existential geopolitical struggle of the 21st century.

When America is taken out of the equation and in a state of collapse, the New Europe will find itself facing domination by Asia and in its third year will launch a massive attack on the Asian association.

Daniel 11:44 But tidings out of the east and out of the north shall trouble him [the New Europe]: therefore he shall go forth with great fury to destroy, and utterly to make away many.

The Asian nations will be prepared and will absorb the blow, after which they will counterattack against the New Europe and its allies.

Many major European military industrial centers will be devastated. Then a vast army from Asia will begin advancing towards Europe.

This will cause the political and religious leaders to move to Jerusalem.

Daniel 11:45 And he shall plant the tabernacles of his palace between the seas in the glorious holy mountain; yet he shall come to his end, and none shall help him.

When these two leaders move to Jerusalem the Asian armies will wheel south and pass through the countries of Psalm 83 who are allied with the New Europe.

Turkey, Syria, Lebanon, Arabia, Jordan, Gaza and Palestine will be overrun and devastated by a huge Asian army of unimaginable numbers, which will then mass before Jerusalem to destroy the two leaders of the New Europe and their last stronghold at Jerusalem.

The Armies of Asia Attack Jerusalem

At this point in the early part of the fourth year, the resurrection of the dead takes place and Christ takes them to the Father's throne in heaven, (Rev 15, Rev 19) for the marriage of the Lamb, while the seven last plagues are poured out.

The sixth plague opens up the way for the armies of Asia to wheel south and sweep through the Middle East to surround Jerusalem where the miracle working false prophet and the political leader are holed up with their remaining forces at Jerusalem.

Not all Jews have yet been deported and a significant number of Jews also remain in the city while large numbers of Palestinians, Jordanians, Europeans and others also remain in the city.

Revelation 16:12 And **the sixth angel** poured out his vial upon the great river Euphrates; and the water thereof was dried up, that the way of the kings of the east might be prepared.

As the Euphrates dries up demons go forth to encourage these armies to turn south to Jerusalem to confront the coming Christ. Of course these are lying spirits and may be saying that a final blow can be struck against the beast in Jerusalem where he has taken refuge; or any similar thing.

16:13 And I saw three unclean spirits like frogs come out of the mouth of the dragon, and out of the mouth of the beast, and out of the mouth of the false prophet.

16:14 For they are the spirits of devils, working miracles, which go forth unto the kings of the earth and of the whole world, to gather them to the battle of that great day of God Almighty.

Outside Jerusalem an Asian army in the tens of millions is massed and at the ready for the final assault.

Revelation 9:16 And the number of the army of the horsemen [soldiers] were two hundred thousand thousand [200 million]: and I heard the number of them.

The entire army from Asia is put at 200 million men, however they will be deployed across the entire region and not all of them will be massed immediately outside Jerusalem.

Now Christ declares that when he comes to rule over all the earth WITH his resurrected saints he will destroy rebellion and wickedness and rule the earth in righteousness. This is not referring to the resurrection of the bride which already happened as the seventh trump began to sound.

These viols of plagues are poured out while the wedding feast is taking place in heaven after the resurrection, and before Christ comes with them to rule the earth.

Blessed is the one who is watching and living by every Word of God!

Revelation 16:15 Behold, I come [with his resurrected chosen to rule; surprising the wicked] as a thief. Blessed is he that watcheth, and keepeth his garments, lest he walk naked, and they see his shame.

16:16 And he gathered them together into a place called in the Hebrew tongue Armageddon.

Now the seventh angel pours out his viol and Christ comes WITH his saints and a mighty earthquake!

Zechariah 14:2 For I will gather all nations against Jerusalem to battle; and the city shall be taken, and the houses rifled, and the women ravished;

and half of the city shall go forth into captivity, and the residue of the people shall not be cut off from the city.

14:3 Then shall the LORD go forth, and fight against those nations, as when he fought in the day of battle.

14:4 And his feet shall stand in that day upon the mount of Olives, which is before Jerusalem on the east, and the mount of Olives shall cleave in the midst thereof toward the east and toward the west, and there shall be a very great valley; and half of the mountain shall remove toward the north, and half of it toward the south.

14:5 And ye shall flee to the valley of the mountains; for the valley of the mountains shall reach unto Azal: yea, ye shall flee, like as ye fled from before the earthquake in the days of Uzziah king of Judah: and the LORD my God shall come, and all the saints with thee.

14:6 And it shall come to pass in that day, that the light shall not be clear, nor dark: **14:7** But it shall be one day which shall be known to the LORD, not day, nor night: but it shall come to pass, that at evening time it shall be light.

Revelation 16:17 And the seventh angel poured out his vial into the air; and there came a great voice out of the temple of heaven, from the throne, saying, It is done.

16:18 And there were voices, and thunders, and lightnings; and there was a great earthquake, such as was not since men were upon the earth, so mighty an earthquake, and so great.

16:19 And the great city was divided into three parts, and the cities of the nations fell: and great Babylon came in remembrance before God, to give unto her the cup of the wine of the fierceness of his wrath.

16:20 And every island fled away, and the mountains were not found.

16:21 And there fell upon men a great hail out of heaven, every stone about the weight of a talent: and men blasphemed God because of the plague of the hail; for the plague thereof was exceeding great.

The Coming of Messiah the Christ

Paul tells us that Christ will come to resurrect those who have died in Christ, and along with the dead he will change those that are alive in Christ [filled with Christ-like zeal to live by EVERY WORD of GOD] giving them new incorruptible bodies made of spirit: at the last [seventh] Trump of Revelation.

1 Thessalonians 4:16 For the Lord himself shall descend from heaven with a shout, with the voice of the archangel, and **with the trump of God**: and the dead in Christ shall rise first:

4:17 Then we which are alive and remain shall be caught up together with them in the clouds, to meet the Lord in the air: and so shall we ever be with the Lord.

Jesus Christ reveals to us that it is when the seventh Trump BEGINS to sound that the resurrection to spirit of the chosen will take place.

Revelation 10:5 And the angel which I saw stand upon the sea and upon the earth lifted up his hand to heaven,

10:6 And sware by him that liveth for ever and ever, who created heaven, and the things that therein are, and the earth, and the things that therein are, and the sea, and the things which are therein, **that there should be time no longer:**

10:7 But in the days of the voice of the seventh angel, when he shall begin to sound, the mystery of God should be finished, as he hath declared to his servants the prophets.

Daniel writes that from the time that the miracle working abomination is set up doing miracles there will be 1290 days; and then tells us that all who reach the 1335 days will be blessed.

Daniel 12:11 And from the time that the daily sacrifice shall be taken away, and the abomination that maketh desolate set up, there shall be a thousand two hundred and ninety days.

12:12 Blessed is he that waiteth, and cometh to the thousand three hundred and five and thirty days.

12:13 But go thou thy way till the end be: for thou shalt rest, and stand in thy lot at the end of the days.

Since we know that after the seventh angel begins to sound the seventh trumpet the seven last plagues must still be poured out and that will take some time, it is obvious that the seven last plagues are poured out on the earth after the resurrection to spirit at the end of the 1,290 days; while the saints are gathered before the throne of God for the Marriage of the Lamb.

Revelation 15:1 And I saw another sign in heaven, great and marvellous, **seven angels having the seven last plagues**; for in them is filled up the wrath of God.

15:2 And I saw as it were a sea of glass mingled with fire: **and them that had gotten the victory over the beast, and over his image, and over his mark, and over the number of his name, stand on the sea of glass, having the harps of God**

The interpretation of the 1290 - 1335 days is that the resurrection to spirit will take place and those changed will ascend to heaven for the Marriage of the Lamb after 1,290 days. Then during the period between the 1290 and the 1335 days the seven last plagues will be poured out on the earth.

Once these plagues are poured out Christ will come to the earth with his collective bride to put down all rebellion against God, to restrain Satan and his demons for a thousand years and to rule all nations. That explains the difference between the 1290 and the 1335 days.

Marriage, making a man and his wife one flesh for life, is an allegory of the unity of spirit that God wants between his people and himself for all eternity. We achieve such unity of spirit with God the Father and Jesus Christ by internalizing their very nature, through enthusiastic study and obedience to all the teachings, law and will of God.

Zechariah 14
The Day of the Lord's coming

The armies of Europe and her allies of Psalm 83 will take Jerusalem at the start of the tribulation and hold it for 42 months, during which period of time many of Judah in Jerusalem will be deported from the city, while many of the Jewish population of Jerusalem will still remain in the city.

Zechariah 14:1 Behold, the day of the Lord cometh, and thy spoil [the spoil of the armies devastated by Christ] shall be divided in the midst of thee.

14:2 For I will gather all nations [of Asia will go up to fight the remaining army of Europe at Jerusalem] against Jerusalem to battle [at the end of the tribulation]; and the city [Yes the whole city of Jerusalem shall be trodden down of the Gentiles for 42 months, Rev 11:2; and then the armies of Asia will come.] shall be taken, and the houses rifled, and the women ravished; and **half of the city shall go forth into captivity, and the residue of the people shall not be cut off from the city.**

Then at the end of 42 months Christ will come with his resurrected chosen and deliver Jerusalem, Judah and Israel!

14:3 Then shall the Lord go forth, and fight against those nations, as when he fought in the day of battle.

Christ shall come WITH his chosen and they will stand on the Mount of Olives and a great earthquake will split the Mount so that the people can flee the battle.

14:4 And **his feet shall stand in that day upon the mount of Olives,** which is before Jerusalem on the east, and the mount of Olives shall cleave in the midst thereof toward the east and toward the west, and there shall be a very great valley; and half of the mountain shall remove toward the north, and half of it toward the south.

14:5 And ye shall flee to the valley of the mountains; for the valley of the mountains shall reach unto Azal: yea, ye shall flee, like as ye fled from before the earthquake in the days of Uzziah king of Judah: and the LORD my God shall come, and all the saints with thee.

This day will be one of dark cloud and the gloominess of battle, and the light of the Eternal shall brighten that night and the day.

14:6 And it shall come to pass in that day, that the light shall not be clear, nor dark:

14:7 But it shall be one day which shall be known to the LORD, not day, nor night: but it shall come to pass, **that at evening time it shall be light.**

These Living Waters are a picture of the flowing of the Holy Spirit from the throne of God to all people.

14:8 And it shall be in that day, that **living waters shall go out from** [the temple site] **Jerusalem**; half of them toward the former sea, and half of them toward the hinder sea: in summer and in winter shall it be.

> **Ezekiel 47** Afterward he brought me again unto the door of the house [the Ezekiel Temple]; and, behold, waters issued out from under the threshold of the house eastward: for the forefront of the house stood toward the east, and the waters came down from under from the right side of the house, at the south side of the altar. Read the whole chapter.

Zechariah 14:9 And **the LORD shall be king over all the earth**: in that day shall there be one LORD [Yahweh], and his name one.

14:10 All the land shall be turned as a plain from Geba to Rimmon south of Jerusalem: and it shall be lifted up [as a plateau] , and inhabited in her place, from Benjamin's gate unto the place of the first gate, unto the corner gate, and from the tower of Hananeel unto the king's winepresses.

14:11 And **men shall dwell in it, and there shall be no more utter destruction; but Jerusalem shall be safely inhabited.**

The armies of Asia which come up against Jerusalem will be consumed.

Revelation 14:19 And the angel thrust in his sickle into the earth, and gathered the vine of the earth, and cast it into the great winepress of the wrath of God. **14:20** And the winepress was trodden without the city, and blood came out of the winepress, even unto the horse bridles, by the space of a thousand and six hundred furlongs [200 miles].

Zechariah 14:12 And this shall be the plague wherewith the LORD will smite all the people that have fought against Jerusalem; **Their flesh shall consume away while they stand upon their feet, and their eyes shall consume away in their holes, and their tongue shall consume away in their mouth.**

14:13 And it shall come to pass in that day, that a great tumult [overwhelming panic and terror] from the LORD shall be among them; and **they shall lay hold every one on the hand of his neighbour, and his hand shall rise up against the hand of his neighbour**.

When God has destroyed these armies, the men of Judah will mop up and take the spoils

14:14 And **Judah also shall fight at Jerusalem;** and the wealth of all the heathen round about shall be gathered together, gold, and silver, and apparel, in great abundance.

Even the animals of the invaders will be destroyed.

14:15 And so shall be the plague of the horse, of the mule, of the camel, and of the ass, and of all the beasts that shall be in these tents, as this plague.

Then ALL nations shall repent and shall know the Eternal.

God will pour out his Spirit on all flesh on the Feast of Pentecost after the end of the 1335 days; so that even the natures of the wild beasts will be changed. The pouring out of God's Spirit on a few thousand on Pentecost in 31 A.D. being only a small precursor to the coming fulfillment.

Joel 2:28 And it shall come to pass afterward, that I will pour out my spirit upon all flesh; and your sons and your daughters shall prophesy, your old men shall dream dreams, your young men shall see visions:

2:29 And also upon the servants and upon the handmaids in those days will I pour out my spirit.

2:30 And I will shew wonders in the heavens and in the earth, blood, and fire, and pillars of smoke.

2:31 The sun shall be turned into darkness, and the moon into blood, before the great and terrible day of the LORD come.

2:32 And it shall come to pass, that whosoever shall call on the name of the LORD shall be delivered: for in mount Zion and in Jerusalem shall be deliverance, as the LORD hath said, and in the remnant whom the LORD shall call.

Zechariah 14:16 And it shall come to pass, that **every one that is left of all the nations which came against Jerusalem shall even go up from year to year to worship the King, the LORD of hosts, and to keep the feast of tabernacles.**

And all flesh shall observe God's seventh day Sabbath [sunset Friday to sunset Saturday] and the New Moons.

> **Isaiah 66:23** And it shall come to pass, that **from one new moon to another, and from one sabbath to another, shall all flesh come to worship before me, saith the Lord.**

Zechariah 14:17 And it shall be, that whoso will not come up of all the families of the earth unto Jerusalem to worship the King, the LORD of hosts, even upon them shall be no rain.

14:18 And if the family of Egypt go not up, and come not, that have no rain; there shall be the plague, wherewith the LORD will smite the heathen that come not up to keep the feast of tabernacles.

Keeping the Sabbath and the New Moons is reckoned with keeping the Feast of Tabernacles! Jesus Christ the King will require these three things in the millennium!

Why do supposedly converted leaders and brethren reject the sanctity of the Sabbath and High Days buying in restaurants and otherwise polluting the Sabbath and High Days, and reject the new moons today? Why do they condemn those who are zealous in these things which God obviously wants us to do? Because they are NOT godly men! They make the commandments of God of no effect by the false traditions of men!

14:19 This shall be the punishment of Egypt, and the punishment of all nations that come not up to keep the feast of tabernacles.

14:20 In that day shall there be upon the bells of the horses, HOLINESS UNTO THE LORD; and the pots in the LORD's house shall be like the bowls before the altar.

The pots shall be holy that the sacrifice of the peace offerings may be cooked in them. For there shall be peace between man and the Eternal God!

14:21 Yea, every pot in Jerusalem and in Judah shall be holiness unto the LORD of hosts: and all they **that sacrifice shall come and take of them, and seethe therein**: and in that day there shall be no more the Canaanite [No more sin, for the Canaanite was a allegorical type of sin.] in the house of the LORD of hosts.

The Millennium

Pentecost: God's Spirit Poured Out On All Flesh

On the Feast of Pentecost at Sinai, the law was written on tables of stone, and in 31 A.D. the law of God was officially written on the hearts of flesh of the called out!

On a near future Pentecost the law of God will be written on the hearts of all mankind then living. This will begin the New Covenant with Israel and will then be extended to all humanity as all mankind then living is grafted into a kind of spiritual Israel and the new and spiritual covenant with Christ.

Jeremiah 31:31 Behold, the days come, saith the LORD, that I will make a new covenant with the house of Israel, and with the house of Judah: **31:32** Not according to the covenant that I made with their fathers in the day that I took them by the hand to bring them out of the land of Egypt; which my covenant they brake, although I was an husband unto them, saith the LORD:

31:33 But this shall be the covenant that I will make with the house of Israel; After those days, saith the LORD, I will put my law in their inward parts, and write it in their hearts; and will be their God, and they shall be my people. **31:34** And they shall teach no more every man his neighbour, and every man his brother, saying, Know the LORD: **for they shall all know me, from the least of them unto the greatest of them, saith the LORD: for I will forgive their iniquity, and I will remember their sin no more.**

Jeremiah was not alone for Ezekiel wrote the word and promise of God saying:

Ezekiel 11:17 Therefore say, Thus saith the Lord GOD; I will even gather you from the people, and assemble you out of the countries where ye have been scattered, and I will give you the land of Israel. **11:18** And they shall come thither, and they shall take away all the detestable things thereof and all the abominations thereof from thence.

11:19 And I will give them one heart, and I will put a new spirit within you; and I will take the stony heart out of their flesh, and will give them an heart of flesh: 11:20 That they may walk in my statutes, and keep mine ordinances, and do them: and they shall be my people, and I will be their God.

The Pentecost of 31 A.D. was about the giving of the Holy Spirit to a small number in an official and public manner; writing the Word of God on the hearts of the called out and fulfilling the promise of the New Covenant; as a type of God's Spirit being poured out on all flesh on a future Feast of Pentecost.

On a near future Pentecost the Holy Spirit of the New Covenant will be poured out on Israel and on all flesh, writing the Word of God on the hearts of all mankind still living and establishing the Kingdom of God, Joel 2:27-28.

We have become confused by considering ourselves first fruits and not understanding that those called during the Millennium [after the resurrection to spirit] are also first fruits; for the seventh day is still part of the same week of first fruits!

During the Millennium, humanity will be called out and have God's Spirit poured out on them, writing the Word of God on their hearts; and they will be changed to spirit or destroyed at 100 years old; thus completing the full seven thousand year harvest of first fruits. Then after the millennium comes the main harvest.

We can now see how this is coming about;

Acts 2:1-4 and when the day of Pentecost was fully come, they were all with one accord or one mind, in one place. And suddenly there came a sound from heaven as of a rushing mighty wind, and it filled all the house where they were sitting. And there appeared unto them cloven tongues like as of fire, and it sat upon each of them. And they were all filled with the Holy Ghost, and began to speak with other tongues, other languages, as the Spirit gave them utterance.

The Spirit of God, is a gift from God; the gift of God's very nature, truth and mind; that we might be enabled to keep the law of God which is a spiritual law.

Romans 7:14 For we know that the law is spiritual:

When we have repented and turned away from sin [which is breaking and compromising with God's Word], we can then be reconciled to God by the application of the sacrifice of Christ; then God can give his nature to those reconciled to him, so that they may internalize his mind, nature, commandments, spirit and actions; writing them on the hearts of humanity.

This spirit is NOT a person; and however various people choose to describe it; it is NOT something that we whip up for ourselves. Otherwise the disciples would not have need of it to be given to them, having already been taught the things of God directly by Christ. [Surely, in their zeal for Christ, they could have whipped up the spirit for themselves if that were possible.]

Acts 2:5 And there were dwelling at Jerusalem Jews, devout men, out of every nation under heaven. **2:6** Now, when this was noised about, the multitude came together, and were confounded.

They were astonished because every person heard them speaking in his own language. These people were not speaking some gobbledygook or babbling away in some spastic emotional ecstasy. They were speaking in the languages of men, and it was being heard in the languages of all the earth; in the genuine languages of men. People were hearing God's word preached to them in their own language.

2:7 And they were all amazed and marveled, saying one to another, Behold, are not all these which speak Galileans? **2:8** And how hear we every man in our own tongue, our own language wherein we were born? **2:9** Parthians, and Medes, and Elamites and the dwellers of Mesopotamia, and in Judaea, and Cappadocia, in Pontus, and Asia, and many others including Cretes and Arabians and Romans.

Acts 2:11 we do hear them speak in our [language] tongues the wonderful works and deeds of God. And they were all amazed, and were in doubt, saying one to another: What does this mean? Well, some mocking said, these men are full of new wine.

But Peter, standing up with the 11, [The apostles: The total of 12 including Peter.], lifted up his voice, and said unto them, You men of Judaea, and all you that dwell at Jerusalem, be this known unto you, and hearken to my words: For these are not drunken, as you suppose, being it is about the third hour of the day, which by the reckoning of the time would be about 9am. But this is that which was spoken by the prophet Joel. And Peter now quoting Joel 2:28, spoke, and it shall come to pass in the last days, saith God, I will pour out of my Spirit upon all flesh.

At this Feast of Pentecost, in 31 A.D.: Was God's Spirit poured out on all flesh? No it was not!

Does all flesh have God's Spirit today? No they don't. What is Peter talking about?

Peter then quotes Joel 2:28, and the events in Acts, were a down payment, an earnest; a first little bit to demonstrate to everyone that this was still going to happen in the future. A little bit then, a lot more in the future.

This prophecy regarding Joel 2:28; that God will put out his spirit on all flesh has still to be fulfilled was fulfilled only in part on the day of Pentecost in the first century where Peter was speaking.

Peter quotes Joel and I will show wonders in heaven above and signs in the earth beneath, blood, and fire, and vapor and smoke. The sun shall be turned into darkness, and the moon into blood, before the great and notable day of the Lord come. And it shall come to pass, that whosoever shall call upon the name of the eternal shall be saved.

Did this happen in the first century? In the days of Peter, did the moon turn to blood? Were all of these signs and wonders done in Peter's day? No, they were not.

This is a prophecy about the last days, the end of the age and of the day of the Lord. When the day of the Lord is over and the Kingdom of God is established; He will pour out his Spirit upon all flesh.

Which is why the lion will lie down with the lamb and the child shall play on the hole of the serpent because all flesh, that's not even just human beings but all flesh will be given a spirit of peace and calmness. And the very nature of all creatures including man and also the vicious beast will be changed into a nature, a peaceable nature.

If we turn now to Daniel 12, we will find that the angel is telling Daniel that from the time that the abomination, the false prophet is set up; from the time he takes his office and he is empowered to do great miracles there shall be 1290 days.

Then, those who have reached the 1335 days shall be blessed, and Daniel shall stand in his lot; receive his responsibility and inheritance.

How are they blessed? Evil is put down. Satan is removed and God's Spirit is poured out on all flesh on the Feast of Pentecost so that the Word of God can be written on the hearts of mankind, according to Joel 2:28, Ezekiel 11:19 and Jeremiah 31.

On a near future Feast of Pentecost God will pour out his Spirit on all flesh and establish his kingdom on the earth, ushering in a period of 1000 years of peace and prosperity unknown to mankind before that time.

A wonderful period; a Millennial Sabbath of rest from Satan and all evil for the all humanity; In which all people shall be called out to become the Millennial Sabbath first fruits, and have God's Spirit poured out on them, and have the Word of God written on their hearts instead of on tables of stone!

There shall be rest from Satan, rest from sin, rest from wickedness. And all people shall enjoy and rejoice with their God, and the faithful shall be changed to spirit at the age of 100 years.

Isaiah 65:20 There shall be no more thence an infant of days, nor an old man that hath not filled his days: **for the child shall die an hundred years old; but the sinner being an hundred years old shall be accursed.**

The Mosaic Covenant was entered into between God and Israel on the Feast of First Fruits, the Feast of Pentecost.

In that Covenant, the law of God was written on tables of Stone, and physical Israel having hearts of flint and not of flesh could not keep the Word of God in its spirit and intent.

This was only a fore-type of the spiritual New Covenant of Jer 31:31 which will also begin on the Feast of Pentecost between God and physical Israel; into which all the Gentiles will be grafted.

We find this in **Acts 5:32** and we are his witnesses of these things; and so is also the Holy Spirit, whom God hath given to those that obey him.

The Holy Spirit is given to those who obey God.

And spiritual things are spiritually discerned as it says in **1 Corinthians 2:14 the** natural, normal, carnal man receiveth not the things of the Spirit of God: for the things of God are foolishness unto them: neither can they know them or understand them, because such things are spiritually discerned.

We must have God's Spirit in order to discern the things of God.

Yes, there is a New Covenant. It is a covenant, as Paul writes in Hebrews, where God will place his law in our hearts and in our minds.

It is a covenant where there is atonement, a sacrifice for sin, which actually does fulfill the need for a complete and total spiritual redemption and deliverance from sin: enabling us then to turn away from our wickedness, to turn toward God, to start keeping his commandments. And in so doing, we can be filled with the Holy Spirit of God.

The Kingdom of God will be set up on the same Feast of Pentecost as the Mosaic theocracy was set up, because God has promised that we shall receive our inheritance over the earth at the end of the days.

Daniel 12:12 Blessed is he that waiteth, and cometh to the thousand three hundred and five and thirty days. **12:13** But go thou thy way till the end be: for thou shalt rest, and stand in thy lot [inheritance] at the end of the days.

This new beginning is pictured by the Feast of Pentecost, the 50th day, being the first day after seven days times seven weeks. It is a new beginning on this day, the Feast of First Fruits, the Feast of Pentecost, and there will be a new beginning on this earth for mankind; with God's Spirit poured out on all flesh (Joel 2:28).

Yes, there will be a Millennium of peace. And that government, that New Covenant of the writing of God's Word on our hearts will be extended and expanded to include all mankind on the Feast of First Fruits.

Zechariah 14:16 And it shall come to pass, that **every one that is left of all the nations which came against Jerusalem shall even go up from year to year to worship the King, the L**ORD** of hosts, and** to keep the feast of tabernacles.

Zechariah 8:20 Thus saith the LORD of hosts; It shall yet come to pass, that there shall come people, and the inhabitants of many cities: **8:22** And the inhabitants of one city shall go to another, saying, Let us go speedily to pray before the LORD, and to seek the LORD of hosts: I will go also.

8:22 Yea, **many people and strong nations shall come to seek the L**ORD** of hosts in Jerusalem, and to pray before the L**ORD**.**

8:23 Thus saith the LORD of hosts; In those days it shall come to pass, that ten men shall take hold out of all languages of the nations, even shall take hold of the skirt of him that is a Jew, saying, We will go with you: for we have heard that God is with you.

Just as a certain amount of God's Spirit was poured out on a few people on that first century day of Pentecost, God's Spirit will be poured out in fullness on all people, on the same day, the same day of Pentecost in the future, after all evil is stamped out and removed.

The Feast of Pentecost is much more than a picture of the official start of the New Covenant.

Pentecost is also the memorial of the start of the Mosaic Covenant of stone; it is a memorial of the beginning of the New Covenant of writing the Word of God on our hearts and circumcising our hearts of stone to turn them into hearts of flesh by the dwelling of Christ in our hearts through his Spirit.

Finally it is also prophetic, looking forward to the establishment of the New Covenant and the writing of the Word of God on the hearts of all flesh then living, after the coming of Jesus Christ with his saints and the establishment of the Kingdom of God over all the earth.

The Millennial Kingdom of God

Jesus Christ will resurrect his faithful and change them to spirit and then he will take them to the Marriage of the Lamb in heaven where they will be instructed further (Rev 15, Rev 19).

Over the next days the seven last plagues will be poured out and when that process has completed Jesus Christ will come to the earth WITH his elect to put down all wickedness and to rule the earth in godly righteousness.

When he returns with his resurrected chosen he will totally destroy the Babylonian Mysteries system.

Then he will wait until the Feast of Pentecost and on that Feast the Kingdom of God will be established and the Holy Spirit will be poured out on all flesh.

The nations, freed from the deception of Satan and humbled, will seek out the Light of the LORD, and as they do so the whole earth will be abundantly blessed. God will pour out his Spirit upon all flesh and all shall know him.

Even the very nature of the wild beasts will be changed to a peaceable and the land shall be healed and become abundantly fruitful.

Isaiah 2:2 And it shall come to pass in the last days, that the mountain [government] of the LORD's house shall be established in the top of the mountains [above all other governments], and shall be exalted above the hills [local governments]; and **all nations shall flow unto it.**

2:3 And **many people shall go and say, Come ye, and let us go up to the mountain of the LORD, to the house of the God of Jacob; and he will teach us of his ways, and we will walk in his paths: for out of Zion shall go forth the law, and the word of the LORD from Jerusalem.**

2:4 And he shall judge among the nations, and shall rebuke many people: and they shall beat their swords into plowshares, and their spears into pruninghooks: nation shall not lift up sword against nation, neither shall they learn war any more.

2:5 O house of Jacob, come ye, and let us walk in the light of the LORD.

Messiah the Christ

Isaiah 9:6 For unto us a child is born, unto us a son is given: and the government shall be upon his shoulder: and his name shall be called Wonderful, Counsellor, The mighty God, The everlasting Father, The Prince of Peace.

9:7 Of the increase of his government and peace there shall be no end, upon the throne of David, and upon his kingdom, to order it, and to establish it with judgment and with justice from henceforth even for ever. The zeal of the LORD of hosts will perform this.

Isaiah 11:1 And there shall come forth a rod out of the stem of Jesse, and a Branch shall grow out of his roots:

11:2 And the spirit of the LORD shall rest upon him, the spirit of wisdom and understanding, the spirit of counsel and might, the spirit of knowledge and of the fear of the LORD;

11:3 And shall make him of quick understanding in the fear of the LORD: and he shall not judge after the sight of his eyes, neither reprove after the hearing of his ears:

11:4 But with righteousness shall he judge the poor, and reprove with equity for the meek of the earth: and he shall smite the earth: with the rod of his mouth, and with the breath of his lips shall he slay the wicked.

11:5 And righteousness shall be the girdle of his loins, and faithfulness the girdle of his reins.

11:6 The wolf also shall dwell with the lamb, and the leopard shall lie down with the kid; and the calf and the young lion and the fatling together; and a little child shall lead them.

11:7 And the cow and the bear shall feed; their young ones shall lie down together: and the lion shall eat straw like the ox.

11:8 And the sucking child shall play on the hole of the asp, and the weaned child shall put his hand on the cockatrice' den.

11:9 They shall not hurt nor destroy in all my holy mountain: for the earth shall be full of the knowledge of the LORD, as the waters cover the sea.

Psalm 67:1 God be merciful unto us, and bless us; and cause his face to shine upon us; Selah.

67:2 That thy way may be known upon earth, thy saving health among all nations.

67:3 Let the people praise thee, O God; let all the people praise thee.

67:4 O let the nations be glad and sing for joy: for thou shalt judge the people righteously, and govern the nations upon earth. Selah.

67:5 Let the people praise thee, O God; let all the people praise thee.

67:6 Then shall the earth yield her increase; and God, even our own God, shall bless us.

67:7 God shall bless us; and all the ends of the earth shall fear him.

Psalm 72:2 He shall judge thy people with righteousness, and thy poor with judgment.

72:3 The mountains shall bring peace to the people, and the little hills, by righteousness.

72:4 He shall judge the poor of the people, he shall save the children of the needy, and shall break in pieces the oppressor.

72:5 They shall fear thee as long as the sun and moon endure, throughout all generations.

72:6 He shall come down like rain upon the mown grass: as showers that water the earth.

72:7 In his days shall the righteous flourish; and abundance of peace so long as the moon endureth.

72:8 He shall have dominion also from sea to sea, and from the river unto the ends of the earth.

72:9 They that dwell in the wilderness shall bow before him; and his enemies shall lick the dust.

72:10 *The kings of Tarshish and of the isles shall bring presents: the kings of Sheba and Seba shall offer gifts.*

72:11 Yea, all kings shall fall down before him: all nations shall serve him

Blessings on the earth

Isaiah 35:1 The wilderness and the solitary place shall be glad for them; and the desert shall rejoice, and blossom as the rose.

35:2 It shall blossom abundantly, and rejoice even with joy and singing: the glory of Lebanon shall be given unto it, the excellency of Carmel and Sharon, they shall see the glory of the LORD, and the excellency of our God.

35:3 Strengthen ye the weak hands, and confirm the feeble knees.

35:4 Say to them that are of a fearful heart, Be strong, fear not: behold, your God will come with vengeance [upon oppressors and the wicked], even God with a recompence; he will come and save you.

35:5 Then the eyes of the blind shall be opened, and the ears of the deaf shall be unstopped.

35:6 Then shall the lame man leap as an hart, and the tongue of the dumb sing: for in the wilderness shall waters break out, and streams in the desert.

35:7 And the parched ground shall become a pool, and the thirsty land springs of water: in the habitation of dragons, where each lay, shall be grass with reeds and rushes.

35:8 And an highway shall be there, and a way [towards true godliness], and it shall be called The way of holiness; the unclean [sinful and unrepentant] shall not pass over it; but it shall be for those: the wayfaring men, though fools, shall not err therein.

35:9 No lion shall be there, nor any ravenous beast shall go up thereon [no evil shall befall the repentant seeking the righteousness of God], it shall not be found there; but the redeemed shall walk there:

35:10 And the ransomed of the LORD shall return, and come to Zion with songs and everlasting joy upon their heads: they shall obtain joy and gladness, and sorrow and sighing shall flee away.

Messiah the Christ; Mighty to Deliver

Isaiah 40:1 Comfort ye, comfort ye my people, saith your God.

40:2 Speak ye comfortably to Jerusalem, and cry unto her, that her warfare is accomplished, that her iniquity is pardoned: for she hath received of the LORD's hand double for all her sins.

40:3 The voice of him that crieth in the wilderness, Prepare ye the way of the LORD, make straight in the desert a highway for our God.

40:4 Every valley shall be exalted, and every mountain and hill shall be made low: and the crooked shall be made straight, and the rough places plain:

40:5 And the glory of the LORD shall be revealed, and all flesh shall see it together: for the mouth of the LORD hath spoken it.

40:6 The voice said, Cry. And he said, What shall I cry? All flesh is grass, and all the goodliness thereof is as the flower of the field:

40:7 The grass withereth, the flower fadeth: because the spirit of the LORD bloweth upon it: surely the people is grass.

40:8 The grass withereth, the flower fadeth: but the word of our God shall stand for ever.

40:9 O Zion, that bringest good tidings, get thee up into the high mountain; O Jerusalem, that bringest good tidings, lift up thy voice with strength; lift it up, be not afraid; say unto the cities of Judah, Behold your God!

40:10 Behold, the Lord GOD will come with strong hand, and his arm shall rule for him: behold, his reward is with him, and his work before him.

40:11 He shall feed his flock like a shepherd: he shall gather the lambs with his arm, and carry them in his bosom, and shall gently lead those that are with young.

40:12 Who hath measured the waters in the hollow of his hand, and meted out heaven with the span, and comprehended the dust of the earth in a measure, and weighed the mountains in scales, and the hills in a balance?

40:13 Who hath directed the Spirit of the LORD, or being his counsellor hath taught him?

40:14 With whom took he counsel, and who instructed him, and taught him in the path of judgment, and taught him knowledge, and shewed to him the way of understanding?

40:15 Behold, the nations are as a drop of a bucket, and are counted as the small dust of the balance: behold, he taketh up the isles as a very little thing.

40:16 And Lebanon is not sufficient to burn, nor the beasts thereof sufficient for a burnt offering.

40:17 All nations before him are as nothing; and they are counted to him less than nothing, and vanity.

40:18 To whom then will ye liken God? or what likeness will ye compare unto him?

40:19 The workman melteth a graven image, and the goldsmith spreadeth it over with gold, and casteth silver chains.

40:20 He that is so impoverished that he hath no oblation chooseth a tree that will not rot; he seeketh unto him a cunning workman to prepare a graven image, that shall not be moved.

40:21 Have ye not known? have ye not heard? hath it not been told you from the beginning? have ye not understood from the foundations of the earth?

40:22 It is he that sitteth upon the circle of the earth, and the inhabitants thereof are as grasshoppers; that stretcheth out the heavens as a curtain, and spreadeth them out as a tent to dwell in:

40:23 That bringeth the princes to nothing; he maketh the judges of the earth as vanity.

Isaiah 60:1 Arise, shine; for thy light is come, and the glory of the LORD is risen upon thee.

60:2 For, behold, the darkness shall cover the earth, and gross darkness the people: but the [light of Messiah] LORD shall arise upon thee, and his glory shall be seen upon thee.

60:3 And **the Gentiles shall come to thy light, and kings to the brightness of thy rising.**

60:4 Lift up thine eyes round about, and see: all they gather themselves together, they come to thee: thy sons shall come from far, and thy daughters shall be nursed at thy side.

60:5 Then thou shalt see, and flow together, and thine heart shall fear, and be enlarged; because the abundance of the sea shall be converted unto thee, the forces of the Gentiles shall come unto thee.

60:6 The multitude of camels shall cover thee, the dromedaries of Midian and Ephah; all they from Sheba shall come: they shall bring gold and incense; and they shall shew forth the praises of the LORD.

60:7 All the flocks of Kedar shall be gathered together unto thee, the rams of Nebaioth shall minister unto thee: they shall come up with acceptance on mine altar, and I will glorify the house of my glory.

60:8 Who are these that fly as a cloud, and as the doves to their windows?

60:9 Surely the isles shall wait for me, and the ships of Tarshish first, to bring thy sons from far, their silver and their gold with them, unto the name of the LORD thy God, and to the Holy One of Israel, because he hath glorified thee.

60:10 And the sons of strangers shall build up thy walls, and their kings shall minister unto thee: for in my wrath I smote thee, but in my favour have I had mercy on thee.

60:11 Therefore thy gates shall be open continually; they shall not be shut day nor night; that men may bring unto thee the forces of the Gentiles, and that their kings may be brought.

60:12 For the nation and kingdom that will not serve [Messiah] thee shall perish; yea, those nations shall be utterly wasted.

60:13 The glory of Lebanon shall come unto thee, the fir tree, the pine tree, and the box together, to beautify the place of my sanctuary; and I will make the place of my feet glorious.

60:14 The sons also of them that afflicted thee shall come bending unto thee; and all they that despised thee shall bow themselves down at the soles of thy feet; and they shall call thee; The city of the LORD, The Zion of the Holy One of Israel.

60:15 Whereas thou has been forsaken and hated, so that no man went through thee, I will make thee an eternal excellency, a joy of many generations.

60:16 Thou shalt also suck the milk of the Gentiles, and shalt suck the breast of [be nourished by the gifts of kings] kings: and **thou shalt know that I the LORD am thy Saviour and thy Redeemer, the mighty One of Jacob.**

60:17 For brass I will bring gold, and for iron I will bring silver, and for wood brass, and for stones iron: I will also make thy officers peace, and thine exactors righteousness.

60:18 Violence shall no more be heard in thy land, wasting nor destruction within thy borders; but thou shalt call thy walls Salvation, and thy gates Praise.

60:19 The sun shall be no more thy light by day; neither for brightness shall the moon give light unto thee: but the LORD shall be unto thee an everlasting light, and thy God thy glory.

The Earth Rejoices at the Coming of the LORD

Psalm 97:1 The LORD reigneth; let the earth rejoice; let the multitude of isles be glad thereof.

97:2 Clouds and darkness are round about him: righteousness and judgment are the habitation of his throne.

97:3 A fire goeth before him, and burneth up his enemies round about.

97:4 His lightnings enlightened the world: the earth saw, and trembled.

97:5 The hills melted like wax at the presence of the LORD, at the presence of the Lord of the whole earth.

97:6 The heavens declare his righteousness, and all the people see his glory.

97:7 Confounded be all they that serve graven images, that boast themselves of idols: worship him, all ye gods.

97:8 Zion heard, and was glad; and the daughters of Judah rejoiced because of thy judgments, O LORD.

97:9 For thou, LORD, art high above all the earth: thou art exalted far above all gods.

97:10 Ye that love the LORD, hate evil: he preserveth the souls of his saints; he delivereth them out of the hand of the wicked.

97:11 Light is sown for the righteous, and gladness for the upright in heart.

97:12 Rejoice in the LORD, ye righteous; and give thanks at the remembrance of his holiness.

Psalm 98:1 O sing unto the LORD a new song; for he hath done marvellous things: his right hand, and his holy arm, hath gotten him the victory.

98:2 The LORD hath made known his salvation: his righteousness hath he openly shewed in the sight of the heathen.

98:3 He hath remembered his mercy and his truth toward the house of Israel: all the ends of the earth have seen the salvation of our God.

98:4 Make a joyful noise unto the LORD, all the earth: make a loud noise, and rejoice, and sing praise.

98:5 Sing unto the LORD with the harp; with the harp, and the voice of a psalm.

98:6 With trumpets and sound of cornet make a joyful noise before the LORD, the King.

98:7 Let the sea roar, and the fulness thereof; the world, and they that dwell therein.

98:8 Let the floods clap their hands: let the hills be joyful together

98:9 Before the LORD; for he cometh to judge the earth: with righteousness shall he judge the world, and the people with equity.

Psalm 99:1 The LORD reigneth; let the people tremble: he sitteth between the cherubims; let the earth be moved.

99:2 The LORD is great in Zion; and he is high above all the people.

99:3 Let them praise thy great and terrible name; for it is holy.

99:4 The king's strength also loveth judgment; thou dost establish equity, thou executest judgment and righteousness in Jacob.

99:5 Exalt ye the LORD our God, and worship at his footstool; for he is holy.

99:6 Moses and Aaron among his priests, and Samuel among them that call upon his name; they called upon the LORD, and he answered them.

99:7 He spake unto them in the cloudy pillar: they kept his testimonies, and the ordinance that he gave them.

99:8 Thou answeredst them, O LORD our God: thou wast a God that forgavest them, though thou tookest vengeance of their inventions.

99:9 Exalt the LORD our God, and worship at his holy hill; for the LORD our God is holy.

Psalm 100:1 Make a joyful noise unto the LORD, all ye lands.

100:2 Serve the LORD with gladness: come before his presence with singing.

100:3 Know ye that the LORD he is God: it is he that hath made us, and not we ourselves; we are his people, and the sheep of his pasture.

100:4 Enter into his gates with thanksgiving, and into his courts with praise: be thankful unto him, and bless his name.

100:5 For the LORD is good; his mercy is everlasting; and his truth endureth to all generations.

The End of Satan

Just before the Kingdom of God is established and God's Spirit is poured out on all flesh on a future Feast of Pentecost, Satan must be restrained and removed from influencing humanity.

The history of man deceived by Satan into deciding right and wrong for himself and doing things his own way has been written in blood. Finally after 3 1/2 years of intense bloodshed and horror when at least one third and probably much more of humanity has died in that one time period, humanity will have been humbled and will be ready to listen to their Father in heaven.

After the whole of Europe and the Middle East as well as much of Asia and most of the rest of the world has been devastated by the wars of men, Messiah the Christ will come to Jerusalem with his chosen changed to spirit elect; and the deceived armies shall turn to fight Christ at his coming.

These armies gathered at Jerusalem will be totally destroyed and hearing of that; all peoples will fear and tremble and run to accept Messiah the Christ as King of kings of the whole earth.

Then only one final task remains to bring the nations to sincere wholehearted acceptance of Christ to live by EVERY WORD of God which will at last bring peace and prosperity to all peoples.

The Great Deceiver must be removed and restrained from deceiving the nations into rebellion against the only way that brings peace and prosperity.

When he comes, Christ will destroy the religious and political leaders of the New Europe and will then restrain Satan and his evil spirits for one thousand years.

Once the deception has been lifted, a humbled humanity which has had its pride ground to contrition will sincerely repent to go forward and "Sin No More" living from then onward, by EVERY WORD of Almighty God!

With Satan removed and the Messiah ruling the whole earth with his now changed to spirit faithful; humanity will wholeheartedly repent to serve God.

At that time Satan the deceiver will be removed and the people will see the power of God which has resurrected the dead in Christ and they will know that, they too, can be resurrected to spirit and given eternal life if they are faithful.

That promise will be much more than words to them, for they will see it fulfilled before their very eyes in the resurrected elect!

After Satan is removed and the people turn to the Eternal, and when the Feast of Pentecost is fully come; God will pour out his Spirit on all flesh!

Joel 2:28 And it shall come to pass afterward [After Christ has come with awesome wonders and removed Satan, and the people have turned to the Eternal], **that I will pour out my spirit upon all flesh**; and your sons and your daughters shall prophesy, your old men shall dream dreams, your young men shall see visions:

2:29 And also upon the servants and upon the handmaids in those days will I pour out my spirit.

2:30 And I will shew wonders in the heavens and in the earth, blood, and fire, and pillars of smoke.

2:31 The sun shall be turned into darkness, and the moon into blood, before the great and terrible day of the LORD come.

2:32 And it shall come to pass, that whosoever shall call on the name of the LORD shall be delivered: for in mount Zion and in Jerusalem shall be deliverance, as the LORD hath said, and in the remnant whom the LORD shall call.

Revelation 20:1 And I saw an angel come down from heaven, having the key of the bottomless pit and a great chain in his hand.

20:2 And he laid hold on the dragon, that old serpent, which is the Devil, and Satan, and **bound him a thousand years**,

20:3 And cast him into the bottomless pit, and shut him up, and set a seal upon him, **that he should deceive the nations no more, till the thousand years should be fulfilled:** and after that he must be loosed a little season.

The resurrected spring harvest of the faithful will reign over the earth working hard to bring in those living during that time into the resurrection to eternal life.

20:4 And I saw thrones, and they sat upon them, and judgment was given unto them: and I saw the souls of them that were beheaded for the witness of Jesus, and for the word of God, and which had not worshipped the beast, neither his image, neither had received his mark upon their foreheads, or in their hands; and **they lived and reigned with Christ a thousand years.**

Only AFTER this one thousand years are the rest of the dead resurrected, therefore the resurrection and judgement of the rest of the dead comes AFTER the Millennium.

20:5 But the rest of the dead lived not again until the thousand years were finished. This is the first resurrection.

20:6 Blessed and holy is he that hath part in the first resurrection: on such the second death hath no power, but they shall be priests of God and of Christ, and s**hall reign with him a thousand years.**

Satan was restrained just before the Feast of Pentecost, which means that he will be released when his thousand years are completed just before the Feast of Pentecost.

20:7 And when the thousand years are expired, Satan shall be loosed out of his prison,

This period of Satanic deception and the destruction of those so deceived is the short space between the First and the Seventh months, with the victory near to the Feast of Trumpets the first day of the seventh month.

After which Satan is judged and removed forever on the Fast of Atonement.

Only after that, does the resurrection to physical life and the Feast of Ingathering [Tabernacles] judgement of all who have lived not knowing God take place.

20:8 And shall go out to deceive the nations which are in the four quarters of the earth, Gog, and Magog, to gather them together to battle: the number of whom is as the sand of the sea.

The Main Harvest of humanity after the Millennium

The great victory over Satan beginning the seventh month

20:9 And they went up on the breadth of the earth, and compassed the camp of the saints about, and the beloved city: and fire came down from God out of heaven, and devoured them.

Satan will be judged and removed forever on the Fast of Atonement

20:10 And the devil that deceived them was cast into the lake of fire and brimstone, where the beast and the false prophet are, and shall be tormented day and night for ever and ever.

Only then, AFTER the Millennium, AFTER Satan is released and deceives again, AFTER the deceived are killed in this final battle; only AFTER the final judgement and removal of Satan, does the Feast of Tabernacles come!

Only then will the Ezekiel 37 resurrection of all humanity who died in ignorance take place, when they will have their opportunity to enter into the Family of God in the Great Judgement of the Feast of Tabernacles

20:11 And I saw a great white throne, and him that sat on it, from whose face the earth and the heaven fled away; and there was found no place for them.

The promise of a resurrection to flesh for Israel, which is extended to all nations in the Feast of Tabernacles instructions

Also see the "Biblical Festivals" books

Ezekiel 37:1 The hand of the LORD was upon me, and carried me out in the spirit of the LORD, and set me down in the midst of the valley which was full of bones, **37:2** And caused me to pass by them round about: and, behold, there were very many in the open valley; and, lo, they were very dry.

37:3 And he said unto me, Son of man, can these bones live? And I answered, O Lord GOD, thou knowest. **37:4** Again he said unto me, Prophesy upon these bones, and say unto them, O ye dry bones, hear the word of the LORD.

37:5 Thus saith the Lord GOD unto these bones; Behold, I will cause breath to enter into you, and ye shall live: **37:6** And I will lay sinews upon you, and will bring up flesh upon you, and cover you with skin, and put breath in you, and ye shall live; and ye shall know that I am the LORD.

37:7 So I prophesied as I was commanded: and as I prophesied, there was a noise, and behold a shaking, and the bones came together, bone to his bone. **37:8** And when I beheld, lo, the sinews and the flesh came up upon them, and the skin covered them above: but there was no breath in them.

37:9 Then said he unto me, Prophesy unto the wind, prophesy, son of man, and say to the wind, Thus saith the Lord GOD; Come from the four winds, O breath, and breathe upon these slain, that they may live. **37:10** So I prophesied as he commanded me, and the breath came into them, and they lived, and stood up upon their feet, an exceeding great army.

37:11 Then he said unto me, Son of man, these bones are the whole house of Israel: behold, they say, Our bones are dried, and our hope is lost: we are cut off for our parts.

37:12 Therefore prophesy and say unto them, Thus saith the Lord GOD; Behold, O my people, I will open your graves, and cause you to come up out of your graves, and bring you into the land of Israel.

37:13 And ye shall know that I am the LORD, when I have opened your graves, O my people, and brought you up out of your graves, **37:14** And shall put my spirit in you, and ye shall live, and I shall place you in your own land: then shall ye know that I the LORD have spoken it, and performed it, saith the LORD.

The same promise of a resurrection to flesh and an opportunity to know God has been made to all other peoples as well.

Satan has deceived the whole world and is ultimately responsible for the wickedness in the world since he has deceived people into rebellion against God.

Daniel 2: Babylon the Great Totally Destroyed

Babylon the Great, pictured by the Statue of Daniel 2 will be utterly destroyed by Christ at his coming.

The head of gold is the Babylonian Empire of Nebuchadnezzar. The breast of silver is the Medo-Persian Empire which replaced Babylon but maintained the same church state system. Then the belly of brass was the Grecian Empire of Alexander which took over from the Medo-Persian Empire and still maintained the same Babylonian system.

These empires were followed by the Roman Empire, and the seven revivals of the Holy Roman Empire, the final revival being ten European rulers who give their military and foreign affairs to one political leader at the behest of a miracle working false prophet.

This final revival of the Holy Roman Empire by whatever name it will be called, will consist of ten nations and be a mixture of brittleness and malleability.

Daniel 2:1 And in **the second year of the reign of Nebuchadnezzar** [c. 605 BC – 562 B.C. the 2nd year would have been in 603 B.C.] Nebuchadnezzar dreamed dreams, wherewith his spirit was troubled, and his sleep brake from him.

The king seeks an answer from the wise men, the spiritualists and false religions of Babylon, and Daniel was not among them.

2:2 Then the king commanded to call the magicians, and the astrologers, and the sorcerers, and the Chaldeans, for to shew the king his dreams. So they came and stood before the king.

The king demands that they not only interpret his dream, but that they describe to him the dream which he had dreamed.

2:3 And the king said unto them, I have dreamed a dream, and my spirit was troubled to know the dream.

2:4 Then spake the Chaldeans to the king in Syriack, O king, live for ever: tell thy servants the dream, and we will shew the interpretation.

The king demands they tell him what he had dreamed and its meaning on pain of death.

2:5 The king answered and said to the Chaldeans, The thing is gone from me: if ye will not make known unto me the dream, with the interpretation thereof, ye shall be cut in pieces, and your houses shall be made a dunghill.

2:6 But if ye shew the dream, and the interpretation thereof, ye shall receive of me gifts and rewards and great honour: therefore shew me the dream, and the interpretation thereof.

They ask the king his dream again, in fear of their lives.

2:7 They answered again and said, Let the king tell his servants the dream, and we will shew the interpretation of it.

2:8 The king answered and said, I know of certainty that ye would gain the time, because ye see the thing is gone from me.

2:9 But if ye will not make known unto me the dream, there is but one decree for you: for ye have prepared lying and corrupt words to speak before me, till the time be changed: therefore tell me the dream, and I shall know that ye can shew me the interpretation thereof.

These spiritualists [Satanists] give their defense, that they simply cannot know such a thing.

2:10 The Chaldeans answered before the king, and said, There is not a man upon the earth that can shew the king's matter: therefore there is no king, lord, nor ruler, that asked such things at any magician, or astrologer, or Chaldean.

2:11 And it is a rare thing that the king requireth, and there is none other that can shew it before the king, except the gods, whose dwelling is not with flesh.

Then the king decrees that all the wise men be killed, and the word comes to Daniel for although worshipers of God and not of the magicians of Babylon; Daniel and his friends are also considered wise men and therefore among those to be killed.

2:12 For this cause the king was angry and very furious, and commanded to destroy all the wise men of Babylon.

2:13 And the decree went forth that the wise men should be slain; and **they sought Daniel and his fellows to be slain**.

Daniel asks why he must die? and is told the reason.

2:14 Then Daniel answered with counsel and wisdom to Arioch the captain of the king's guard, which was gone forth to slay the wise men of Babylon:

2:15 He answered and said to Arioch the king's captain, Why is the decree so hasty from the king? Then Arioch made the thing known to Daniel.

Then Daniel informs the king that he will inquire of God and tell him the dream and its interpretation. We can see that this was set up by God to reveal to Nebuchadnezzar that the God of Daniel is God indeed, and that the gods of the Babylonian mysteries were not gods at all.

It is the Eternal who is God above all gods and it is wickedness to inquire of the false gods and the Babylonian Mysteries.

2:16 Then Daniel went in, and desired of the king that he would give him time, and that he would shew the king the interpretation.

Then Daniel and his friends inquired of the Eternal.

2:17 Then Daniel went to his house, and made the thing known to Hananiah, Mishael, and Azariah, his companions:

2:18 That they would desire mercies of the God of heaven concerning this secret; that Daniel and his fellows should not perish with the rest of the wise men of Babylon.

The Eternal God revealed the dream to Daniel.

It is the Eternal to whom we should go for understanding, and anyone who seeks support for his own false suppositions from the writings of false religions will fall into the same ditch of ignorance that such false teachers are in; and will reap the same correction for the wickedness of seeking understanding of spiritual things from demons.

2:19 Then was the secret revealed unto Daniel in a night vision. Then Daniel blessed the God of heaven.

Daniel gives all praise and glory to the Eternal alone; for the Eternal alone is the source of all wisdom and truth; not Satan and his ministers!

Daniel's prayer of thanksgiving to the Eternal for giving him the understanding, which has saved the lives of all God's faithful in the king's service.

2:20 Daniel answered and said, Blessed be the name of God for ever and ever: for wisdom and might are his:

2:21 And he changeth the times and the seasons: he removeth kings, and setteth up kings: he giveth wisdom unto the wise, and knowledge to them that know understanding:

2:22 He revealeth the deep and secret things: he knoweth what is in the darkness, and the light dwelleth with him.

2:23 I thank thee, and praise thee, O thou God of my fathers, who hast given me wisdom and might, and hast made known unto me now what we desired of thee: for thou hast now made known unto us the king's matter.

Daniel went to Arioch who seems to have been very reluctant to carry out the king's orders and desirous to save the lives of the wise men.

2:24 Therefore Daniel went in unto Arioch, whom the king had ordained to destroy the wise men of Babylon: he went and said thus unto him; Destroy not the wise men of Babylon: bring me in before the king, and I will shew unto the king the interpretation.

2:25 Then **Arioch brought in Daniel before the king in haste**, and said thus unto him, I have found a man of the captives of Judah, that will make known unto the king the interpretation.

The king asks Daniel if he can reveal the dream.

2:26 The king answered and said to Daniel, whose name was Belteshazzar, Art thou able to make known unto me the dream which I have seen, and the interpretation thereof?

Daniel answers the king.

2:27 Daniel answered in the presence of the king, and said, The secret which the king hath demanded cannot the wise men, the astrologers, the magicians, the soothsayers, shew unto the king;

2:28 But **there is a God in heaven that revealeth secrets,** and maketh known to the king Nebuchadnezzar **what shall be in the latter days.**

God alone gives understanding of the things of God including the Word of God and the dreams and visions sent by God: Not the ignorant followers of Satan.

Anyone who imagines his own interpretations and then seeks out support for them from the writings of the heathen and the followers of Satan in the Babylonian Mysteries, is spiritually blind and no prophet of God.

Daniel then tells the king his dram and the interpretation. The dream is a prophecy of the future of the kingdom of Babylon.

. . . Thy dream, and the visions of thy head upon thy bed, are these;

2:29 As for thee, O king, thy thoughts came into thy mind upon thy bed, what should come to pass hereafter: and he that revealeth secrets maketh known to thee what shall come to pass.

Daniel declares that the understanding is given to him from God and not for any wisdom of his own.

Like Daniel I say, if I have been right in any thing it is from God and not from any wisdom of mine. I am no better than any other; indeed I am less than nothing. Give ALL glory to the Eternal who reveals his wisdom unto worldly babes who put their complete trust in him!

2:30 But as for me, this secret is not revealed to me for any wisdom that I have more than any living, but for their sakes that shall make known the interpretation to the king, and that thou mightest know the thoughts of thy heart.

The dream

2:31 Thou, O king, sawest, and behold a great image. This great image, whose brightness was excellent, stood before thee; and the form thereof was terrible.

2:32 This image's head was of fine gold, his breast and his arms of silver, his belly and his thighs of brass,

2:33 His legs of iron, his feet part of iron and part of clay.

2:34 Thou sawest till that a stone was cut out without hands, which smote the image upon his feet that were of iron and clay, and brake them to pieces.

2:35 Then was the iron, the clay, the brass, the silver, and the gold, broken to pieces together, and became like the chaff of the summer threshingfloors; and the wind carried them away, that no place was found for them: and the stone that smote the image became a great mountain, and filled the whole earth.

Later, king Nebuchadnezzar was to make a replica of this dream image and demand that all should worship it.

The interpretation

2:36 This is the dream; and we will tell the interpretation thereof before the king.

God gave the kingdom of Babylon to Nebuchadnezzar; He and the kingdom that he built in Babylon are the head of gold.

2:37 Thou, O king, art a king of kings: for **the God of heaven hath given thee a kingdom, power, and strength, and glory.**

2:38 And wheresoever the children of men dwell, the beasts of the field and the fowls of the heaven hath he given into thine hand, and hath made thee ruler over them all. **Thou art this head of gold.**

The breast of silver was the empire of the Medes and Persians which was dominated by the Medes with the advent of king Darius. The Medes and Persians took over the Babylonian empire (539 B.C.) but maintained the same Babylonian church state governance system intact. The people changed, the system remained the same; therefore the different kingdoms were each still a part of the Babylonian system as the different metals were still a past of the same statue.

The third kingdom of brass was the same Babylonian system now taken over from the Medes and Persians by the Greeks

2:39 And after thee shall arise another kingdom inferior to thee, and another third kingdom of brass, which shall bear rule over all the earth.

The fourth part of the image was of iron, but still the same statue; the Babylonian Mysteries church state system. The iron representing Rome and its powerful military.

2:40 And the fourth kingdom shall be strong as iron: forasmuch as iron breaketh in pieces and subdueth all things: and as iron that breaketh all these, shall it break in pieces and bruise.

The feet and toes of the statue of Babylon, picture the church state Holy Roman Empire with its own seven revivals (Rev 17).

The whole statue was of the Babylonian system and each succeeding empire although led by a different people maintained the same Babylonian Mysteries church state system.

This system is called Babylon the Great, and a final revival of the church state Holy Roman Empire [regardless of what it is named]; A New European federal system including ten nations will soon rise up and come back to life for the final time; to be destroyed and replaced by the coming Messiah the Christ.

2:41 And whereas thou sawest the feet and toes, part of potters' clay, and part of iron, the kingdom shall be divided; but there shall be in it of the strength of the iron, forasmuch as thou sawest the iron mixed with miry clay.

2:42 And as the toes of the feet were part of iron, and part of clay, so the kingdom shall be partly strong, and partly broken [weak].

The strength of Rome will be mingled with weaker peoples in the coming final revival.

2:43 And whereas thou sawest iron mixed with miry clay, they shall mingle themselves with the seed of men: but they shall not cleave one to another, even as iron is not mixed with clay.

The ten toes represent ten rulers who will form this final Babylon system by giving their authority to one leader. Messiah the Christ will come to destroy the Babylonian Mysteries System that the statue represents; and set up the kingdom of God.

> **Revelation 17:12** And the ten horns which thou sawest are ten kings [rulers], which have received no kingdom as yet; but receive power as kings one hour [a short time, 42 months] with the beast. **17:13** These have one mind, and shall give their power and strength unto the beast. **17:14** These shall make war with the Lamb, and the Lamb shall overcome them: for he is Lord of lords, and King of kings: and they that are with him are called, and chosen, and faithful.

Daniel 2:44 And in the days of these kings shall the God of heaven set up a kingdom, which shall never be destroyed: and the kingdom shall not be left to other people, but it shall break in pieces and consume all these kingdoms, and it shall stand for ever.

The Chief Corner Stone [Messiah the Christ] will come down from the mountain of the government of God the Father in heaven.

2:45 Forasmuch as thou sawest that the stone was cut out of the mountain without hands , and that it brake in pieces the iron, the brass, the clay, the silver, and the gold; the great God hath made known to the king what shall come to pass hereafter: and the dream is certain, and the interpretation thereof sure.

2:46 Then the king Nebuchadnezzar fell upon his face, and worshipped Daniel, and commanded that they should offer an oblation and sweet odours unto him.

This whole process and prophecy, revealed to Nebuchadnezzar that the Eternal is God indeed and that the other god's and their servants and priests were as nothing and totally without godly wisdom.

In our day, when Christ comes and this Babylonian system is destroyed, all people will worship God and turn on and destroy the false religions.

> **Revelation 17:16** And the ten horns which thou sawest upon the beast, these shall hate the whore [the false religion which has deceived and dominated them], and shall make her desolate and naked, and shall eat her flesh, and burn her with fire. **17:17** For **God hath put in their hearts to fulfil his will, and to agree, and give their kingdom unto the beast, until the words of God shall be fulfilled.**

Daniel 2:47 The king answered unto Daniel, and said, Of a truth it is, that your God is a God of gods, and a Lord of kings, and a revealer of secrets, seeing thou couldest reveal this secret.

2:48 Then the king made Daniel a great man, and gave him many great gifts, and made him ruler over the whole province of Babylon, and chief of the governors over all the wise men of Babylon.

2:49 Then Daniel requested of the king, and he set Shadrach, Meshach, and Abednego, over the affairs of the province of Babylon: but Daniel sat in the gate of the king.

Jesus Christ will destroy this evil empire along with the armies of Asia gathered at Jerusalem when he comes to the Mount of Olives, and he shall cast this final pope and this political leader into a roaring fire to be totally destroyed.

Revelation 19:19 And I saw the beast, and the kings of the earth, and their armies, gathered together to make war against him [Messiah the Christ] that sat on the horse, and against his army.

19:20 And the beast [European political leader] was taken, and with him the false prophet [miracle working pope] that wrought miracles before him, with which he deceived them that had received the mark of the beast [deciding for themselves what is right and wrong and so rebelling against God], and them that worshipped his image [followed and obeyed that system]. **These both were cast alive into a lake of fire burning with brimstone.**

19:21 And the remnant [of the armies gathered to resist Christ] were slain with the sword of him that sat upon the horse, which sword proceeded out of his mouth [the sword is the Word and will of God proclaimed by the mouth of Christ] : and all the fowls were filled with their flesh.

20:1 And I saw an angel come down from heaven, having the key of the bottomless pit and a great chain in his hand.

20:2 And he laid hold on [Satan and his demons] the dragon, that old serpent, which is the Devil, and Satan, and bound him a thousand years,

Then Satan will also be restrained and the ten rulers, now with their eyes opened, will understand that they have been deceived; and will turn on the Babylonian Mystery religion and destroy it.

Revelation 17:16 And the ten horns which thou sawest upon the beast, these shall hate the whore [false religion], and shall make her desolate and naked, and shall eat her flesh, and burn her with fire.

17:17 For God hath put in their hearts [allowed them to be deceived for a time] to fulfil his will, and to agree, and give their kingdom unto the beast, until the words of God shall be fulfilled.

The Restoration of Israel

After Solomon died his son Rehoboam reigned in his place and because of the sins of Solomon God rent the Ten Tribes of Israel from Rehoboam and Judah and broke the bands of brotherhood between Judah and Israel.

In these latter days God will withdraw his blessings from both Judah and Israel for all their sins and the nations of Israel shall fall with Judah at the same time (Hos 5:5).

After we have been humbled and turned to live by every Word of God, Christ will come and heal the breach between Israel and Judah restoring the brotherhood of Jacob.

The separation of Judah and Israel shall be healed and a representative part of each tribe will return to the physical Promised Land while also keeping the areas to which they have spread like Britain, Canada, America, Scandinavia, the Netherlands and more. Then under the resurrected king David; Homeland Israel shall extend from the River of Egypt to the Euphrates.

When Christ comes and all of humanity repents, the old hatreds will perish out of the earth!

Then deeply repentant, having been humbled by the armies of Asia and delivered by Christ, modern Jordan and Gaza as well as much of Lebanon and Syria shall be incorporated into Israel and shall serve the Eternal in wholehearted zeal.

The resurrected David will rule a once again united Israel and Judah.

Under Christ the resurrected David will rule all of this land as the National Homeland of Israel as well as the modern lands given to the tribes of Israel today.

Hosea 3:5 Afterward shall the children of Israel return, and **seek the Lord their God, and David their king**; and shall fear the Lord and his goodness in the latter days.

When Christ comes, he will set a resurrected David back upon his throne, to rule all Israel FOREVER, thus fulfilling God's promise to David!

Ezekiel 34:23 And I will set up one shepherd over them, and he shall feed them, **even my servant David;** he shall feed them, and he shall be their shepherd. **34:24** And I the Lord will be their God, and my servant David a prince among them; I the Lord have spoken it.

Ezekiel 37:24 And **David my servant shall be king over them**; and they all shall have one shepherd: they shall also walk in my judgments, and observe my statutes, and do them [thus showing that the whole law and every Word of God will also be kept forever!]. **37:25** And they shall dwell in the land that I have given unto Jacob my servant, wherein your fathers have dwelt; and they shall dwell therein, even they, and their children, and their children's children for ever: and my servant David shall be their prince for ever.

After the coming of Christ, Israel will again be united and will turn to the Eternal, and the resurrected David will be king over all Israel; and God's promise of a perpetual Davidic throne over Israel will be fulfilled!

Jeremiah 30:9 But they shall serve the Lord their God, and **David their king, whom I will raise up unto them**.

In the Millennium and under the resurrected David, each of the twelve apostles will have one tribe in Israel to rule.

Matthew 19:27 Then answered Peter and said unto him, Behold, we have forsaken all, and followed thee; what shall we have therefore?

19:28 And Jesus said unto them, Verily I say unto you, That ye which have followed me, in the regeneration when the Son of man shall sit in the throne of his glory, ye also shall sit upon twelve thrones, judging the twelve tribes of Israel.

Each of the twelve apostles will rule over his own tribe in Israel; including both its area in the National Homeland in Palestine and also the area it has been blessed with outside of Palestine.

For example the ruler of Zebulon will rule Zebulon in its National Homeland in Palestine and will also rule its national blessing possession of the Netherlands; and the ruler of Manasseh will rule Manasseh in its National Homeland in Palestine and will also rule its national blessing possession of the United States of America.

David will be king over the twelve apostles and all the tribes of Israel and also rule over the modern lands that the Tribes of Israel have been blessed with.

Jesus Christ will rule all nations of the whole earth and under Christ David will be overall king of all the nations of Israel.

Ezekiel 37:15 The word of the LORD came again unto me, saying,

37:16 Moreover, thou son of man, take thee one stick, and write upon it, For Judah, and for the children of Israel his companions: then take another stick, and write upon it, For Joseph, the stick of Ephraim and for all the house of Israel his companions:

37:17 And join them one to another into one stick; and they shall become one in thine hand.

37:18 And when the children of thy people shall speak unto thee, saying, Wilt thou not shew us what thou meanest by these?

37:19 Say unto them, Thus saith the Lord GOD; Behold, I will take the stick of Joseph, which is in the hand of Ephraim, and the tribes of Israel his fellows, and will put them with him, even with the stick of Judah, and make them one stick, and they shall be one in mine hand.

37:20 And the sticks whereon thou writest shall be in thine hand before their eyes.

37:21 And say unto them, Thus saith the Lord GOD; Behold, I will take the children of Israel from among the heathen, whither they be gone, and will gather them on every side, and bring them into their own land:

37:22 And I will make them one nation in the land upon the mountains of Israel; and one king shall be king to them all: and they shall be no more two nations, neither shall they be divided into two kingdoms any more at all.

37:23 Neither shall they defile themselves any more with their idols, nor with their detestable things, nor with any of their transgressions: but I will save them out of all their dwellingplaces, wherein they have sinned, and will cleanse them: so shall they be my people, and I will be their God.

37:24 And **David my servant shall be king over them; and they all shall have one shepherd: they shall also walk in my judgments, and observe my statutes, and do them.**

37:25 And they shall dwell in the land that I have given unto Jacob my servant, wherein your fathers have dwelt; and they shall dwell therein, even they, and their children, and their children's children for ever: and my servant David shall be their prince for ever.

37:26 Moreover I will make a covenant of peace with them; it shall be an everlasting covenant with them: and I will place them, and multiply them, and will set my sanctuary in the midst of them for evermore.

37:27 My tabernacle also shall be with them: yea, I will be their God, and they shall be my people.

37:28 And the heathen shall know that I the LORD do sanctify Israel, when my sanctuary shall be in the midst of them for evermore.

God's unshakable promise of the restoration of Judah and Israel together after they are turned to him in the tribulation; the very reason that God will allow the tribulation is to bring Israel and all nations to him.

Jeremiah 30:1 The word that came to Jeremiah from the LORD, saying,

30:2 Thus speaketh the LORD God of Israel, saying, Write thee all the words that I have spoken unto thee in a book.

30:3 For, lo, the days come, saith the LORD, that I will bring again the captivity of my people Israel and Judah, saith the LORD: and **I will cause them to return to the land that I gave to their fathers, and they shall possess it.**

30:4 And these are the words that the LORD spake **concerning Israel and concerning Judah.**

The Tribulation

30:5 For thus saith the LORD; We have heard a voice of trembling, of fear, and not of peace.

30:6 Ask ye now, and see whether a man doth travail with child? wherefore do I see every man with his hands on his loins, as a woman in travail, and all faces are turned into paleness?

30:7 Alas! for that day is great, so that none is like it: it is even **the time of Jacob's trouble,** but he shall be saved out of it.

Deliverance by the Coming of Messiah

30:8 For it shall come to pass in that day, saith the LORD of hosts, that I will break his yoke [Babylon the New Europe] from off thy neck, and will burst thy bonds, and strangers shall no more serve themselves of him:

30:9 But [When Christ comes] **they shall serve the LORD their God, and David their king,** whom I will raise up [from the dead] unto them.

30:10 Therefore fear thou not, O my servant Jacob, saith the LORD; neither be dismayed, O Israel: for, lo, **I will save thee from afar, and thy seed from the land of their captivity; and Jacob shall return, and shall be in rest, and be quiet, and none shall make him afraid.**

30:11 For I am with thee, saith the LORD, to save thee: though I make a full end of all nations whither I have scattered thee, yet I will not make a full end of thee: but I will correct thee in measure, and will not leave thee altogether unpunished.

30:12 For thus saith the LORD, Thy bruise is incurable, and thy wound is grievous.

30:13 There is none to plead thy cause, that thou mayest be bound up: thou hast no healing medicines.

30:14 All thy lovers [friend's allies] have forgotten thee; they seek thee not; for I have wounded thee with the wound of an enemy, with the chastisement of a cruel one, for the multitude of thine iniquity; because thy sins were increased.

We are afflicted because of our many sins. This affliction is from God and will include all of the wicked on the earth as well

30:15 Why criest thou for thine affliction? thy sorrow is incurable for the multitude of thine iniquity: because thy sins were increased, **I have done these things unto thee.**

30:16 Therefore all they that devour thee shall be devoured; and all thine adversaries, every one of them, shall go into captivity; and they that spoil thee shall be a spoil, and all that prey upon thee will I give for a prey [to correct them for their own wickedness].

30:17 For I will restore health unto thee, and I will heal thee of thy wounds, saith the LORD; because they called thee an Outcast, saying, This is Zion, whom no man seeketh after.

30:18 Thus saith the LORD; Behold, I will bring again the [deliver you out of] captivity of Jacob's tents, and have mercy on his dwellingplaces; and the city [Jerusalem] shall be builded upon her own heap, and the palace shall remain after the manner thereof.

Great Rejoicing at Deliverance

30:19 And out of them shall proceed thanksgiving and the voice of them that make merry: and I will multiply them, and they shall not be few; I will also glorify them, and they shall not be small.

30:20 Their children also shall be as aforetime, and their congregation shall be established before me [in zealous godliness], and I will punish [all of the wicked shall be corrected to humble them and turn them to God as Israel was humbled and turned to God] all that oppress them.

30:21 And their nobles shall be of themselves, and their governor shall proceed from the midst of them [our rulers shall be our own people and not strangers]; and I will cause him to draw near, and he shall approach unto me [we shall be given godly rulers who will rule in righteousness]: for who is this that engaged his heart to approach unto me? saith the LORD.

30:22 And **ye shall be my people, and I will be your God.**

30:23 Behold, the whirlwind of the LORD goeth forth with fury, a continuing whirlwind: **it shall fall with pain upon the head of the wicked.**

30:24 The fierce anger of the LORD shall not return, until he hath [corrected all wickedness in Israel and in the earth] done it, and until he have performed the intents of his heart: in the latter days ye shall consider it.

Jeremiah 31:1 At the same time [when the correction has accomplished the repentance of the people], saith the LORD, **will I be the God of all the families of Israel, and they shall be my people.**

31:2 Thus saith the LORD, The people which were left of the sword found grace [repented] in the wilderness; even Israel, when I went to cause him to rest.

31:3 The LORD hath appeared of old unto me, saying, Yea, I have loved thee with an everlasting love: therefore with lovingkindness have I drawn thee.

31:4 Again I will build thee, and thou shalt be built, O virgin [purified by God] of Israel: thou shalt again be adorned with thy tabrets, and shalt go forth in the dances of them that make merry.

31:5 Thou shalt yet plant vines upon the mountains of Samaria: the planters shall plant, and shall eat them as common things.

31:6 For there shall be a day, that the watchmen upon the mount Ephraim shall cry, **Arise ye, and let us go up to Zion unto the LORD our God.**

31:7 For thus saith the LORD; Sing with gladness for Jacob, and shout among the chief of the nations: publish ye, praise ye, and say, **O LORD, save thy people, the remnant of Israel** [Hebrew: Hosanna].

31:8 Behold, I will bring {Israel and Judah back to their land] them from the north country, and gather them from the coasts of the earth, and with them the blind and the lame, the woman with child and her that travaileth with child together: a great company shall return thither.

31:9 They shall come with weeping [sincere repentance], and with supplications will I lead them: I will cause them to walk by the rivers of waters [symbolic of the Holy Spirit] in a straight way [to live by every Word of God], wherein they shall not stumble: for I am a father to Israel, and Ephraim is my firstborn.

31:10 Hear the word of the LORD, O ye nations, and declare it in the isles afar off, and say, He [God has corrected Israel and God will save them] that scattered Israel will gather him, and keep him, as a shepherd doth his flock.

31:11 For the LORD hath redeemed Jacob, and ransomed him from the hand of him that was stronger than he.

31:12 Therefore they shall come and sing in the height of Zion, and shall flow together to the goodness of the LORD, for wheat, and for wine, and for oil, and for the young of the flock and of the herd: and their soul shall be as a watered garden; and they shall not sorrow any more at all.

31:13 Then shall the virgin rejoice in the dance, both young men and old together: for I will turn their mourning into joy, and will comfort them, and make them rejoice from their sorrow.

31:14 And I will satiate the soul of the priests with fatness [offerings], and my people shall be satisfied with my goodness, saith the LORD.

31:15 Thus saith the LORD; A voice was heard in Ramah, lamentation, and bitter weeping; Rahel weeping for her children [Rachel figuratively weeping because of the great affliction of God's correction] refused to be comforted for her children, because they were not.

31:16 Thus saith the LORD; **Refrain thy voice from weeping, and thine eyes from tears:** for thy work shall be rewarded [Your children will repent and be saved], saith the LORD; and they shall come again from the land of the enemy.

31:17 And there is hope in thine end, saith the LORD, that thy children shall come again to their own border.

31:18 I have surely heard Ephraim [the British peoples] bemoaning [sincerely repenting] himself thus; **Thou hast chastised me, and I was chastised, as a bullock unaccustomed to the yoke: turn thou me, and I shall be turned; for thou art the LORD my God.**

31:19 Surely after that I was turned, I repented; and after that I was instructed, I smote upon my thigh: I was ashamed, yea, even confounded, because I did bear the reproach of my youth.

31:20 Is Ephraim my dear son? is he a pleasant child? for since I spake against him, I do earnestly remember him still: therefore my bowels are troubled for him; I will surely have mercy upon him, saith the LORD.

31:21 Set thee up waymarks, make thee high heaps: set thine heart toward the highway, even the way which thou wentest: turn again [turn to God in sincere repentance that thy prosperity might be restored], O virgin of Israel, turn again to these thy cities.

31:22 How long wilt thou go about [remain astray], O thou backsliding daughter? for the LORD hath created a new thing in the earth, A woman shall compass a man.

31:23 Thus saith the LORD of hosts, the God of Israel; As yet they shall use this speech in the land of Judah and in the cities thereof, when I shall bring again their captivity; [The repentant shall utter this saying] **The LORD bless thee, O habitation of justice, and mountain of holiness.**

31:24 And there shall dwell in Judah itself, and in all the cities thereof together, husbandmen, and they that go forth with flocks.

31:25 For I have satiated the weary soul, and I have replenished every sorrowful soul.

31:26 Upon this I awaked, and beheld; and my sleep was sweet unto me.

31:27 Behold, the days come, saith the LORD, that I will sow the house of Israel and the house of Judah with the seed of man, and with the seed of beast.

31:28 And it shall come to pass, **that like as I have watched over them, to pluck up, and to break down, and to throw down, and to destroy, and to afflict; so will I watch over them, to build, and to plant, saith the LORD.**

31:29 In those days they shall say no more, The fathers have eaten a sour grape, and the children's teeth are set on edge.

31:30 But every one shall die for his own iniquity: every man that eateth the sour grape, his teeth shall be set on edge.

31:31 Behold, **the days come, saith the LORD, that I will make a new covenant with the house of Israel, and with the house of Judah:**

31:32 Not according to the covenant that I made with their fathers in the day that I took them by the hand to bring them out of the land of Egypt; which my covenant they brake, although I was an husband unto them, saith the LORD:

31:33 But **this shall be the covenant that I will make with the house of Israel; After those days** [after the tribulation of correction when Christ comes and the people sincerely repent], **saith the LORD, I will put my law in their inward parts, and write it in their hearts; and will be their God, and they shall be my people.**

31:34 And they shall teach no more every man his neighbour, and every man his brother, saying, Know the LORD: for **they shall all know me, from the least of them unto the greatest of them, saith the LORD: for I will forgive their iniquity, and I will remember their sin no more.**

31:35 Thus saith the LORD, which giveth the sun for a light by day, and the ordinances of the moon and of the stars for a light by night, which divideth the sea when the waves thereof roar; The LORD of hosts is his name:

31:36 If those ordinances depart from before me, saith the LORD, then the seed of Israel also shall cease from being a nation before me for ever.

31:37 Thus saith the LORD; If heaven above can be measured, and the foundations of the earth searched out beneath, I will also cast off all the seed of Israel for all that they have done, saith the LORD.

31:38 Behold, the days come, saith the LORD, that the city [Jerusalem] shall be built to the LORD from the tower of Hananeel unto the gate of the corner.

31:39 And the measuring line shall yet go forth over against it upon the hill Gareb, and shall compass about to Goath.

31:40 And the whole valley of the dead bodies, and of the ashes, and all the fields unto the brook of Kidron, unto the corner of the horse gate toward the east, shall be holy unto the LORD; it shall not be plucked up, nor thrown down any more for ever.

Ezekiel 40 - 48 describes the millennial Jerusalem and the millennial temple.

The 42 month tribulation will begin with Judah and Jerusalem and then spread into the nations of Israel; America, Britain, Canada, Australia, New Zealand, Scandinavia, the Netherlands and Belgium etc.

Then the tribulation will expand to include ALL nations on the earth. Humanity will be humbled and brought to repentance so that Messiah the Christ can come and pour the Holy Spirit out on ALL flesh (Joel 2:28)! And all nations will be grafted into the New Covenant as a kind of spiritual Israel!

Germany, Austro-Hungary [Assyria]

INTRODUCTION: Nineveh was the capital of the Assyrian Empire and this prophecy against Nineveh and Assyria [modern Germany, Austria and Hungary] is for the ancients and the latter day Babylon.

Today's modern Assyrian nations of Germany, Austria and Hungary will be the head [the main strength] of the soon coming New Europe.

As the head controls the whole body so the capital city controls and therefore represents the whole nation. Therefore this prophecy of Nineveh is about all of Assyria and in modern terms the whole German Austro-Hungarian people of today.

The prophecy is dual, some of it was fulfilled in the past and some of it is to be fulfilled in the near future.

Daniel 8:23 And in the latter time of their kingdom, when the transgressors are come to the full, a king of fierce countenance, and understanding dark sentences [the occult (spiritualism and witchcraft) and also highly technical things], shall stand up.

8:24 And his power shall be mighty, but not by his own power [his power will come from fallen spirits and the occult]: and he shall destroy wonderfully [to an awesome degree], and shall prosper, and practise, and shall destroy the mighty and the holy people.

8:25 And through his policy also he shall cause craft to prosper in his hand; and he shall magnify himself in his heart [great pride], and by peace [shall attack in a time of peace] shall destroy many: he shall also stand up against the Prince of princes [Messiah the Christ when he comes]; but he shall be broken without hand [By Messiah the Christ when he comes, Dan 2].

The prophecy is about latter day Germanic peoples as the descendants of Nineveh and Assyria, who will be the chief nations of the New Europe which is the feet of the image of Babylon the Great of Dan 2.

Assyria is not only modern Germany but also the nations of Austria and Hungary.

To this day Europeans call Germany Allemagne or some derivative and the Alemanni were the chief tribe of Assyria.

Hungary Hun-Gary [Hun Land] is a land given to the Huns by the Romans to keep them out of Rome.

It is certainly clear that Germany, Austria, Hungary and France will be the core of the New Europe; possibly joined by the overwhelmingly Catholic countries of Italy, Spain, Poland, the Czech Republic, the Slovak Republic and Portugal.

The prophecy begins with the Might, and Glory of the Eternal; and then chastises the latter day leader of Assyria for his affront against God and God's people, concluding with God's response to all of Assyria [Austro Hungary and Germany] as representing the Babylon of the New Europe; for their pride and for their over zealousness in correcting Israel and the called out of God's people.

In the third year of the correction of Israel this New Europe will go out to attack the nations of Asia who will counterattack destroying the New Europe including the German nations. then Israel shall be delivered by the Almighty.

Isaiah 10:12 Wherefore it shall come to pass, that when the Lord hath performed his whole work upon mount Zion and on Jerusalem, **I will punish the fruit of the stout heart of the king of Assyria, and the glory of his high looks**

10:13 For he saith, By the strength of my hand I have done it, and by my wisdom; for I am prudent: and I have removed the bounds of the people, and have robbed their treasures, and I have put down the inhabitants like a valiant man

10:14 And my hand hath found as a nest the riches of the people: and as one gathereth eggs that are left, have I gathered all the earth; and there was none that moved the wing, or opened the mouth, or peeped.

God used Assyria to humble the nations, and not acknowledging that, they will become filled with pride in what they see as their own achievements

10:15 Shall the axe boast itself against him that heweth therewith? or shall the saw magnify itself against him that shaketh it? as if the rod should shake itself against them that lift it up, or as if the staff should lift up itself, as if it were no wood

10:16 Therefore shall the Lord, the Lord of hosts, send among his fat ones leanness; and under his glory he shall kindle a burning like the burning of a fire

10:17 And the light of Israel shall be for a fire, and his Holy One for a flame: and it shall burn and devour his thorns and his briers in one day

10:18 And shall consume the glory of his forest [his mighty men], and of his fruitful field, both soul and body: and they **shall be as when a standard-bearer fainteth.**

10:19 And the rest of the trees [his armies of men] of his forest shall be few, that a child may write [count] them

10:20 And it shall come to pass in that day, that the remnant of Israel, and such as are escaped of the house of Jacob, shall no more again stay upon [serve] him that smote them; but shall stay upon [serve] the Lord, the Holy One of Israel, in truth.

10:21 The remnant shall return, even the remnant of Jacob, unto the mighty God.

Nahum 1

Nahum 1:1 The burden of Nineveh [The capitol representing all of Assyria (the Austro Hungarian German people) and their descendants]. The book of the vision of Nahum the Elkoshite.

A warning against those who would attack the called out of God; those called out of physical Egypt or those called out of spiritual Egypt.

1:2 God is jealous, and the LORD revengeth; the LORD revengeth, and is furious; the LORD will take vengeance on his adversaries, and he reserveth wrath for his enemies.

The latter day Germanic nation's leading the New Europe will do the will of God in correcting us for our wickedness, but will then be lifted up with pride thinking that they had done this by their own wisdom and strength. They will overdo and take pleasure in the correction of God's people, and being full of sin themselves will be corrected by the nations of Asia.

The Eternal is Mighty and we would do well to quickly and sincerely repent before him, for he will correct all the wicked.

1:3 The LORD is slow to anger, and great in power, and will not at all acquit the wicked: the LORD hath his way in the whirlwind and in the storm, and the clouds are the dust of his feet.

1:4 He rebuketh the sea, and maketh it dry, and drieth up all the rivers: Bashan languisheth, and Carmel, and the flower of Lebanon languisheth.

1:5 The mountains quake at him, and the hills melt, and the earth is burned at his presence, yea, the world, and all that dwell therein.

1:6 Who can stand before his indignation? and who can abide in the fierceness of his anger? his fury is poured out like fire, and the rocks are thrown down by him.

As the LORD is strong to rebuke and correct the wicked; he is also Mighty to save his faithful who live by his EVERY WORD!

1:7 The LORD is good, a strong hold in the day of trouble; and he knoweth them that trust in him.

Those who put their trust in God and faithfully keep all of his commandments without compromise will never be disappointed by his love, mercy and ultimate deliverance; those who are against him and his beloved will certainly feel his wrath.

1:8 But with an overrunning flood he will make an utter end of the place thereof, and darkness shall pursue his enemies.

God will not allow the New Europe to make an utter and full end of physical and spiritual Israel! No not at all! God will bring us to sincere repentance for our idolatries and the Almighty will then deliver those who turn to HIM!

1:9 What do ye imagine against the LORD? [do you imagine that God will permit you (the New Europe) to totally destroy the nations of Israel?] he will make an utter end: [God will make an end of affliction. No, God will deliver his people once they have been humbled to contrition and will never again afflict them to this degree] affliction shall not rise up the second time.

While the New Europe is rich and satisfied and full of prosperity, drunken with pride; in the third year they shall be devoured like dry stubble by the armies of Asia.

Daniel 11:44 But tidings out of the east and out of the north shall trouble him: therefore he shall go forth with great fury to destroy, and utterly to make away many.

Nahum 1:10 For while they be folden together as thorns, and while they are drunken [with pride] as drunkards, they shall be devoured as stubble fully dry.

1:11 There is one come out of thee [a ruler will yet rise up out of Assyria, the Germanic peoples; possibly an Austro Hungarian], that imagineth evil against the LORD, a wicked counsellor.

A wicked leader who despises God's Word and is deeply into the occult will rise up to rule the New Europe and shall conquer Israel/Judah and many other nations.

1:12 Thus saith the LORD; Though they [physical and spiritual Israel / Judah] be quiet [at peace], and likewise many [though they be very strong] yet thus shall they be cut down, when he [this wicked leader of the New Europe] shall pass through [correct Israel/ Judah and many nations]. [Then God promises us that when we have been humbled and are sincerely repentant he will deliver us] Though I have afflicted thee, I will afflict thee no more.

Once we are humbled to contrition and sincerely repentant the yoke of this oppressor will be broken.

1:13 For now will I break his yoke from off thee, and will burst thy bonds in sunder.

The judgment of this wicked political leader; is that he shall be destroyed along with his idols.

Revelation 19:19 And I saw the beast, and the kings of the earth, and their armies, gathered together to make war against him that sat on the horse, and against his army. **19:20** And the beast was taken, and with him the false prophet that wrought miracles before him, with which he deceived them that had received the mark of the beast, and them that worshipped his image. These both were cast alive into a lake of fire burning with brimstone.

Nahum 1:14 And the LORD hath given a commandment concerning thee, that no more of thy name be sown: out of the house of thy gods will I cut off the graven image and the molten image: I will make thy grave; for thou art vile.

The Eternal will cut off this political leader and the final false prophet and his false religion and will destroy them. Then peace shall be published with the destruction of wickedness; and the nations shall observe the Solemn Feasts of the LORD in Jerusalem with Judah.

1:15 Behold upon the mountains the feet of him that bringeth good tidings, that publisheth peace! O Judah, keep thy solemn feasts, perform thy vows: for the wicked shall no more pass through thee; he is utterly cut off.

Nahum 2

The Asian armies are come up against Assyria [the head of the New Europe] because the correction of Israel is completed and at an end. Now it s Assyria's turn to be corrected for their witchcrafts [occult spiritism] and great pride. The armies of Asia shall surround Jerusalem where this wicked leader has taken refuge with his religious leader.

The destruction of Nineveh as a type of the defeat of Assyrian (the New Europe) at Jerusalem.

Nahum 2:1 He that dasheth in pieces is come up before thy face: keep the munition, watch the way, make thy loins strong, fortify thy power mightily.

God has used the new Europe to correct Israel and many countries and now it is the turn of Assyria and the New Europe to be corrected.

2:2 For the LORD hath turned away the excellency of Jacob, as the excellency of Israel: for the emptiers have emptied them out, and marred their vine branches.

The armies of Asia shall attack Jerusalem where the last army of the new Europe is entrenched and half the city shall be taken, Zechariah 14. Blood will flow greatly in this battle.

2:3 The shield of his mighty men is made red [with blood], the valiant men are in scarlet [covered in blood] : the chariots [vehicles] shall be with flaming torches in the day of his preparation, and the fir trees [mighty men] shall be terribly shaken.

2:4 The chariots [modern military vehicles] shall rage in the streets, they shall justle one against another in the broad ways: they shall seem like torches, they shall run like the lightnings.

These things give us the reason behind Jonah's hatred of Nineveh [Assyria], yet Jonah was forced to act out an allegorical prophecy that after the coming of Christ, the Word of God will go even to Nineveh [the Assyrians] and they will repent just like the ancient city did.

2:5 He shall recount his worthies: they shall stumble in their walk; they shall make haste to the wall thereof, and the defence shall be prepared.

2:6 The gates of the rivers [a type of the latter day armies of Asia flowing to Jerusalem] shall be opened, and the palace shall be dissolved.

2:7 And Huzzab [meaning "established" and refers to the Assyrian army] shall be led away captive, she shall be brought up, and her maids shall lead her as with the voice of doves, tabering upon their breasts [in mourning].

2:8 But Nineveh is of old like a pool of water: yet they shall flee away. Stand, stand, shall they cry; but none shall look back.

The armies of the oppressors will be commanded to stand and fight, but they shall all flee away from the Asian armies. Then Messiah shall come and destroy the armies who resist him to deliver Judah. Then Judah shall flee by the Mount of Olives while their men rise up against the enemy within the city and take a great spoil.

2:9 Take ye the spoil of silver, take the spoil of gold: for there is none end of the store and glory out of all the pleasant furniture.

Despoil your oppressors and empty them of their good things for God is against them.

2:10 She is empty, and void, and waste: and the heart melteth, and the knees smite together, and much pain is in all loins, and the faces of them all gather blackness.

2:11 Where is the dwelling of the lions [the mighty men who devoured Israel / Judah shall be destroyed], and the feedingplace of the young lions, where the lion, even the old lion, walked, and the lion's whelp, and none made them afraid?

2:12 The lion did tear in pieces enough for his whelps, and strangled for his lionesses, and filled his holes with prey, and his dens with ravin.

2:13 Behold, I am against thee, saith the LORD of hosts, and I will burn her chariots in the smoke, and the sword shall devour thy young lions [mighty men]: and I will cut off thy prey from the earth, and the voice of thy messengers shall no more be heard.

Nahum 3

Judgment on Nineveh the capital of Assyria [Austria Hungary Germany being the head of the coming New Europe]. As the head represents the whole body the Capital represents the whole nation.

Nahum 3:1 Woe to the bloody city [Nineveh the capital of Assyria is a type of the soon coming New Europe]! it is all full of lies and robbery; the prey departeth not [The new Europe takes the prey and spoils of many nations];

3:2 The noise of a whip, and the noise of the rattling of the wheels, and of the pransing horses, and of the jumping chariots.

The Assyrian and his empire has killed, torn and devoured like a lion, therefore the sword of the Eternal shall correct him.

3:3 The horseman lifteth up both the bright sword and the glittering spear: and there is a multitude of slain, and a great number of carcases; and there is none end of their corpses; they stumble upon their corpses:

The leader of the soon coming New Europe will be deep into the occult along with the false prophet.

3:4 Because of the multitude of the whoredoms of the wellfavoured harlot, the mistress of witchcrafts, that selleth nations through her whoredoms, and families through her witchcrafts.

3:5 Behold, I am against thee, saith the LORD of hosts; and I will discover thy skirts upon thy face, and I will shew the nations thy nakedness [the wickedness will be revealed], and the kingdoms thy shame.

God corrects all the wicked in his own time.

3:6 And I will cast abominable filth upon thee, and make thee vile, and will set thee as a gazingstock.

3:7 And it shall come to pass, that all they that look upon thee shall flee from thee, and say, Nineveh is laid waste: who will bemoan her? whence shall I seek comforters for thee?

3:8 Art thou better than populous No, that was situate among the rivers, that had the waters round about it, whose rampart was the sea, and her wall was from the sea?

3:9 Ethiopia and Egypt were her strength, and it was infinite; Put and Lubim were thy helpers.

3:10 Yet was she carried away, she went into captivity: her young children also were dashed in pieces at the top of all the streets: and they cast lots for her honourable men, and all her great men were bound in chains.

3:11 Thou also shalt be drunken [with pride]: thou shalt be hid, thou also shalt seek strength [seek help] because of the enemy.

3:12 All thy strong holds shall be like fig trees with the firstripe figs: if they be shaken, they shall even fall into the mouth of the eater.

3:13 Behold, thy people in the midst of thee are [become like helpless] women: the gates of thy land shall be set wide open unto thine enemies: the fire shall devour thy bars.

3:14 Draw thee waters for the siege, fortify thy strong holds: go into clay, and tread the morter, make strong the brickkiln [to build defenses].

3:15 There shall the fire devour thee; the sword shall cut thee off, it shall eat thee up like the cankerworm: make thyself many as the cankerworm, make thyself many as the locusts.

3:16 Thou hast multiplied thy merchants above the stars of heaven: the cankerworm spoileth, and fleeth away.

3:17 Thy crowned are as the locusts [in numbers], and thy captains [are as many as the grasshoppers] as the great grasshoppers, which camp in the hedges in the cold day, but when the sun ariseth they flee away, and their place is not known where they are.

3:18 Thy shepherds slumber, O king of Assyria: thy nobles shall dwell in the dust: thy people is scattered upon the mountains, and no man gathereth them.

3:19 There is no healing of thy bruise; thy wound is grievous: all that hear the bruit of thee shall clap the hands [in rejoicing at thy fall] over thee: for upon whom hath not thy wickedness passed continually [for who has not suffered at your hands?]?

Jonah is an allegorical prophecy that when the Millennium begins and Satan's deception is removed: Nineveh [today's Germanic peoples] will sincerely repent and come to live by EVERY WORD of God!

Egypt

Egypt shall fall with Judah and shall be controlled by the New Europe for 42 months. She shall be freed by the coming of Messiah the Christ and like all nations will wholeheartedly turn to embrace the Eternal.

Isaiah 19:19 In that day [In the Millennium after Messiah comes] **shall there be an altar to the LORD in the midst of the land of Egypt, and a pillar at the border thereof to the LORD.**

19:20 And it shall be for a sign and for a witness unto the LORD of hosts in the land of Egypt: [In the tribulation the Egyptians shall cry out to God for deliverance and shall turn to Messiah the Christ when he comes] for they shall cry unto the LORD because of the oppressors, and he shall send them a saviour [Messiah Jesus Christ (Hebrew: Yeshua)], and a great one, and he [The King of kings Messiah the Christ] shall deliver them.

19:21 And **the LORD shall be known to Egypt, and the Egyptians shall know the LORD in that day, and shall do sacrifice and oblation; yea, they shall vow a vow unto the LORD, and perform it.**

19:22 And the LORD shall smite Egypt: he shall smite [Egypt shall be humbled] and heal it [Then Egypt will turn to God and Christ the King of kings when he comes and the millennium begins]: and they shall return even to the LORD, and he shall be intreated of them, and shall heal them.

19:23 In that day shall there be a highway out of Egypt to Assyria [The German peoples], and the Assyrian shall come into Egypt, and the Egyptian into Assyria, and the Egyptians shall serve [God] with the Assyrians.

19:24 In that day shall Israel be the third with Egypt and with Assyria, even a blessing in the midst of the land [the whole earth]**:**

19:25 Whom the LORD of hosts shall bless, saying, Blessed be Egypt my people, and Assyria the work of my hands, and Israel mine inheritance.

Turkey

The coming regional war in the Middle East will reset regional realities bringing a genuine dialogue for peace and finally a real peace deal.

When peace is declared [1 Thess 5:3] the extremist Jewish Settler Movement will work to sabotage that deal, possibly including staging an attack on the Pope when he visits the temple mount in Jerusalem.

This will bring on the occupation of Jerusalem, Judea and Egypt by **a confederation of Islamic nations under the leadership of Turkey as per Psalm 83 allied with New Europe.**

Gaining control of Judea they will rule with ferocity and will seek to destroy or to thrust as many Jews as possible from off the land.

God has warned throughout the Fifth Book of Moses that possession of the Promised Land is totally dependent on the inhabitants keeping all the commandments of God.

Since modern Jews in Judea do not keep God's commandments and the land is full of abominations, they shall see one final captivity.

The Book of Obadiah is a warning to Turkey that if they ally with the New Europe and afflict Judah; they shall also be destroyed in their turn.

The New Europe shall go forth to attack Asia in the third year of the occupation of Judea, and the Asian nations shall respond crushing Europe and overrunning the Middle East to attack Jerusalem, where the Europeans leaders have fled to make their last stand.

Daniel 11:40 And at the time of the end shall the king of the south [Judah/Egypt] push at him: and the king of the north [the New Europe] shall come against him like a whirlwind, with chariots, and with horsemen, and with many ships; and he shall enter into the countries, and shall overflow and pass over.

Daniel 11:41 He shall enter also into the glorious land [Palestine], and many countries shall be overthrown: but these shall escape out of his hand, even [his allies] Edom [Turkey], and Moab, and the chief of the children of Ammon [Moab and Ammon are modern Jordan].

11:42 He shall stretch forth his hand also upon the countries: and the land of Egypt shall not escape.

11:43 But he shall have power over the treasures of gold and of silver, and over all the precious things of Egypt: and the Libyans and the Ethiopians shall be at his steps [shall serve the New Europe] .

11:44 But tidings out of the east and out of the north [Russia and China] shall trouble him: therefore he shall go forth [in the third year after the occupation of Jerusalem] with great fury to destroy, and utterly to make away many

11:45 And he shall [the rulers of the New Europe will then flee to Jerusalem for their last stand] plant the tabernacles of his palace between the seas in the glorious holy mountain; yet he shall come to his end, and none shall help him.

Obadiah 1:1 The vision of Obadiah. Thus saith the Lord GOD concerning Edom [Modern Turkey]; We have heard a rumour from the LORD, and an ambassador is sent among the heathen [the nations of Asia], Arise ye, and let us rise up against her in battle.

Edom is modern Turkey; who will be in league with the New Europe and the nations surrounding modern Judea [except for Egypt] against Judah, Psalm 83.

1:2 Behold, I have made thee small among the heathen: thou art greatly despised.

1:3 The pride of thine heart hath deceived thee, thou that dwellest in the clefts of the rock, whose habitation is high [Those who live in the mountains of modern Turkey]; that saith in his heart, Who shall bring me down to the ground?

1:4 Though thou exalt thyself as the eagle, and though thou set thy nest among the stars, thence will I bring thee down, saith the LORD.

After the New Europe conquers Judea, the Turks shall think in their heart that as an ally of the New Europe they are safe from all possible enemies and will never fall in their mountainous land.

1:5 If thieves came to thee, if robbers by night, (how art thou cut off!) would they not have stolen till they had enough? if the grape gatherers [reapers] came to thee, would they not leave some grapes?

1:6 How are the things of Esau [Esau is Edom] searched out! how are his hidden things sought up!

1:7 All the men of thy confederacy have brought thee even to the border: the men that were at peace with thee have deceived thee, and prevailed against thee; that they eat thy bread have laid a wound under thee: there is none understanding in him.

Turkey's allies cannot save her and cannot defend her against the massive armies of Asia.

Germany will be a part of the New Europe and in addition to the world's Roman Catholic nations the following Islamic nations will be allied with the New Europe.

Turkey shall ally themselves with the New Europe and their other allies.

> **Psalm 83:1** Keep not thou silence, O God: hold not thy peace, and be not still, O God.
>
> **83:2** For, lo, thine enemies make a tumult: and they that hate thee have lifted up the head.

83:3 They have taken crafty counsel against thy people, and consulted against thy hidden ones.

83:4 They have said, Come, and let us cut them off from being a nation; that the name of Israel may be no more in remembrance.

83:5 For they have consulted together with one consent: they are confederate against thee:

83:6 The tabernacles of Edom [Turkey], and the Ishmaelites [true Arabs, sons of Ishmael; sons of Abraham and Agar]; of Moab [northern Jordan today], and the Hagarenes [Arabs who are sons of Agar (Hagar) by another than Abraham, and also not the sons of Ishmael];

83:7 Geba [Lebanon], and Ammon [southern Jordan today], and Amalek [a tribe of the Turks]; the Philistines [Gaza] with the inhabitants of Tyre;

83:8 Assur [Germany, Austro-Hungary and teh New Europe of Ten Nations] also is joined with them: they have holpen the children of Lot [will help modern Jordan; Ammon and Moab].

Selah.

Obadiah 1:8 Shall I not in that day, saith the LORD, even destroy the wise men out of Edom [Turkey], and understanding out of the mount of Esau [Turkey]?

1:9 And thy mighty men, O Teman [Esau, Turkey], shall be dismayed, to the end that every one of the mount of Esau may be cut off by slaughter.

Turkey shall fall for he shall be given over to the nations of the East for his perfidy against his brother Jacob [all the modern Israelite nations]. All the mighty men of war of Turkey shall be destroyed by the coming Russian / Chinese / Asian counter attack into the Middle East during and after the third year of the captivity of Judah.

Jerusalem shall be trodden down of the Gentles for forty-two months and then shall Messiah come with all his saints; to bring in righteousness and to rule the whole earth.

1:10 For thy violence against thy brother Jacob shame shall cover thee, and thou shalt be cut off for ever.

Turkey cut off from being an independent nation

1:11 In the day that thou stoodest on the other side, in the day that the strangers carried away captive his [Judah's] forces, and foreigners entered into his [Judah's] gates, and cast lots upon Jerusalem, even thou wast as one of them [one of the enemies of Judah].

1:12 But thou shouldest not have looked on the day of thy brother in the day that he became a stranger; neither shouldest thou have rejoiced over the children of Judah in the day of their destruction; neither shouldest thou have spoken proudly in the day of distress.

When the New Europe conquers modern Judah; Turkey shall rejoice and take part in dividing the spoils taken from his brother Judah.

1:13 Thou shouldest not have entered into the gate of my people in the day of their calamity; yea, thou shouldest not have looked on their affliction in the day of their calamity, nor have laid hands on their substance in the day of their calamity;

1:14 Neither shouldest thou have stood in the crossway, to cut off those of his that did escape; neither shouldest thou have delivered up those of his that did remain in the day of distress.

Turkey shall have a part in despoiling Judah

1:15 For the day of the LORD is near upon all the heathen: as thou hast done, it shall be done unto thee: thy reward shall return upon thine own head.

1:16 For as ye have drunk upon my holy mountain, so shall all the heathen drink continually, yea, they shall drink, and they shall swallow down, and they shall be as though they had not been.

In the third year of the occupation of Judea, the New Europe will go to make war with Russia, China and the Shanghai Cooperation Organization and they shall respond by defeating Europe and then invading Turkey and the Middle East, massing outside Jerusalem where the leaders of Europe will have fled to make their last stand.

The armies of Asia shall sweep through and devastate Turkey, the Arab countries, Syria, Lebanon, Gaza and Palestine, and then Messiah the Christ shall come.

All of these Middle East nations including Egypt will have been thoroughly humbled and will rejoice at the coming of Christ and their deliverance; they will sincerely wholeheartedly turn to the Eternal and submit to the leadership of Israel over the entire Middle East under Messiah the King of kings!

When Messiah the Christ comes he will give the land of modern Turkey to Jacob [all Israel].

1:17 But upon mount Zion shall be deliverance, and there shall be holiness; and the house of Jacob shall possess their possessions.

Then shall Messiah come to deliver all Israel and shall destroy all those arrayed against him; and all the nations of Israel shall rise up to take control of the Turkish nation and those nations who have destroyed them.

1:18 And the house of Jacob [Israel] shall be a fire, and the house of Joseph [Ephraim (the British peoples) and Manasseh (the Anglo Saxon Americans)] a flame, and the house of Esau [Turkey] for stubble, and they shall kindle in them, and devour them; and there shall not be any [wicked unrepentant] remaining of the house of Esau; for the LORD hath spoken it.

1:19 And they of the south [Judah] shall possess the mount of Esau [The area of ancient Edom]; and they of the plain [Judah] the Philistines [Gaza]: and they [The Ten Tribes of Israel] shall possess the fields of Ephraim, and the fields of Samaria: and Benjamin [The land of Benjamin is around Jerusalem in the south, yet they shall be given a place in Gilead in the land of Reuben, and Manasseh east of Jordan near Golan] shall possess Gilead.

In that day the nations of Israel shall take Turkey for a vassal and shall be given all of Samaria and Gaza by the Eternal. The ten tribes of Israel shall govern Samaria and Judah shall be in the south in her own land, for the Jews have no right to the land given to the ten tribes.

The removal of the Jews from much of Jerusalem and from much of the land north of Jerusalem by the New Europe and the Psalm 83 alliance, followed by the decimation of the Palestinians by the Asian armies, will clear that land for the ingathering of the ten tribes to their land of Samaria.

Today, Judah considers the Palestinians [who are mainly Samaritans] as Canaanites, because most of them converted to Islam during the spread of that religion. This is a political ploy to make them appear as people to be destroyed by the Jews. The men of Judah have always coveted the land of Samaria and fought many wars with Israel to try and take the land north of Jerusalem.

Palestinians are not Canaanites! They are mainly Samaritans who converted to Islam.

Many Canaanites today live in Lebanon and others are widely spread abroad.

1:20 And the captivity of this host of the children of Israel shall possess that of the Canaanites [Lebanon], even unto Zarephath [Sidon]; and the captivity of Jerusalem, which is in Sepharad [removed to Spain], shall possess the cities of the south.

1:21 And saviours [the resurrected chosen] shall come up on mount Zion to judge the mount of Esau; and the kingdom shall be the LORD's.

The Kingdom of God shall be established by Messiah the Christ, who shall destroy the wicked, and shall rule over the whole earth; and the remnant of the Turkmen people shall wholeheartedly turn to and serve the Eternal.

Then Turkey and the Turkmens shall be confederate with Israel and subject to the resurrected king David.

Amos 9:11 In that day will I raise up the tabernacle of David that is fallen, and close up the breaches thereof; and I will raise up his ruins, and I will build it as in the days of old:

9:12 That they may possess the remnant of Edom [Turkey], and of all the heathen, **which are called by my name** [which have sincerely repented and turned to God], saith the LORD that doeth this.

Key Prophecies

Daniel 8: The 2300 Days

The 2,300 Day Prophecy

Daniel's vision here is dated in the third year of Belshazzar, while the dream of Daniel 7 was dated in the first year if Belshazzar. The events of the Belshazzar period conclude with Daniel 5 and the fall of Babylon.

Daniel 8:1 In the third year of the reign of king Belshazzar a vision appeared unto me, even unto me Daniel, after that which appeared unto me at the first.

8:2 And I saw in a vision; and it came to pass, when I saw, that **I was at Shushan in the palace, which is in the province of Elam; and I saw in a vision, and I was by the river of Ulai.**

A vision is very much like watching a short extremely vivid movie which remains sharply imprinted on one's mind for many years. One sees the vision which is as clear and sharp as the very best film right before one's eyes, while wide awake.

The vision begins with the fall of Babylon to the Medo-Persians

First the vision is given and later in the chapter the explanation is provided. In the hope that it will be helpful I am adding the explanation to the vision.

The Ram

8:3 Then I lifted up mine eyes, and saw, and, behold, there stood before the river **a ram** which had **two horns**: and the **two horns were high; but one was higher than the other, and the higher came up last**.

After Babylon fell it was first ruled by king Cyrus the Persian the first horn, which was succeeded by king Darius the Mede the second horn.

> **Explanation: Daniel 8:20** The **ram which thou sawest having two horns are the kings of Media and Persia.**

Daniel 8:4 I saw the **ram pushing westward, and northward, and southward**; so that no beasts [no other nation] might stand before him, neither was there any that could deliver out of his hand; but he did according to his will, and became great.

The He Goat

8:5 And as I was considering, behold, **an he goat came from the west on the face of the whole earth, and touched not the ground: and the goat had a notable horn between his eyes.**

> **Explanation: Daniel 8:21** And **the rough goat is the king of Grecia**: and the **great horn that is between his eyes is the first king**.

Alexander carried out the plans of his father king Philip of Macedonia, and united the Greeks becoming the first king of a united Greece; after which he conquered Media-Persia.

Alexander Conquers Medo Persia.

8:6 And **he came to the ram that had two horns** [Medo-Persia], which I had seen standing before the river, and ran unto him in the fury of his power.

8:7 And I saw him [the he goat; Alexander's Greek empire] come close unto the ram [The Medo-Persian empire], and he was moved with choler [fury] against him, and **smote the ram, and brake his two horns**: and there was no power in the ram to stand before him, but he cast him down to the ground, and stamped upon him: and there was none that could deliver the ram out of his hand.

8:8 Therefore the **he [Greece, Alexander] goat waxed very great: and when he was strong, the great horn was broken** [Alexander died suddenly at Babylon June 323 B.C.]**; and for it** [the Greek empire] **came up four notable ones** [after infighting by many contenders Alexander's empire was divided into four parts somewhere near 280 B.C.] **toward the four winds** [four directions; north, east, south and west] **of heaven.**

> **Explanation: Daniel 8:22** Now that being broken, whereas four stood up for it, [After Alexander died his empire was ultimately divided into four kingdoms somewhere around 280 B.C.] **four kingdoms shall stand up out of the nation**, but not in his power.

The prophecy tells us that Alexander's empire will be divided into four parts, and then immediately skips to the end time and the the final end time fierce king of the North.

Out of one of these four divisions became the king of the north, and carried on as Babylon historically called Seleucid Syria.

8:9 And **out of one of them** [one of the four, Seleucid Syria called Babylon at that time] **came forth a little horn** [henceforth called the the king [ruler] of the north, became very powerful]**, which waxed exceeding great, toward the south, and toward the east, and toward the pleasant land.**

> **Explanation:** One of these four; the king of the north called Babylon, or Seleucid Syria became very powerful across Syria. Daniel 11 is a history of the competition between this king of the north Seleucid Syria and the king of the south Egypt, over control of Judea Palestine.
>
> Seleucid Syria became a part of the Roman empire in 133 B.C. when the king of Pergamos, Attalus 3, died and willed that kingdom to Rome. At that time Rome assumed the mantel of king of the north continuation of the Babylonian Mysteries System, the iron legs of Daniel 2.
>
> At the final end time "the latter time" of the king of the north; Babylon the Great, the final [seventh] revival of the Holy Roman Empire [by whatever name it is called] will take place and this same

system will once again make war against the king of the South [Egypt and Judea and their allies].

Daniel 8:23 And in the **latter time** [the end time] of their kingdom, **when the transgressors are come to the full, a king of fierce countenance** [intimidating appearance], **and understanding dark sentences** [secret things including complicated technology and evil spiritual powers], **shall stand up** [become ruler of the North, the New European Holy Roman Empire (by whatever name it takes) revival].

8:24 And his power shall be mighty, but not by his own power [he will be supported by Satan's power]: and he shall destroy wonderfully [awesomely], and shall prosper, and practise, and shall destroy the mighty and the holy people.

This final revival of the Holy Roman Empire Babylonian church state system in a New Federal Europe will overcome many beginning in a time of peace and shall be very rich for about two years before attacking Asia in the third year; and later he will attempt to fight the arriving Christ.

8:25 And through his policy also he shall cause craft to prosper in his hand; and he shall magnify himself in his heart, and by peace shall destroy many: **he shall also stand up against the Prince of princes; but he shall be broken without hand.**

The prophecy insets to Satan, of whom this political system and its ruler are a servant and a type. Satan being the one who led one third of the angels in rebellion against God and ascended to try to make war on God.

Daniel 8:10 And it waxed great, even to the host of heaven; and it cast down some of the host and of the stars to the ground, and stamped upon them.

Here this final political [beast] ruler of the last revival of Babylon, the now rising New Federal Europe; is used as an allegory of Satan who fought against the host of heaven and cast some of the stars [angels] to the ground. This kind of allegory is consistent with the Isaiah and Ezekiel verses using men as a type of Lucifer / Satan.

This man will persecute the called out spiritual Ekklesia on the earth and he will fight Christ at his coming, but this man is only a tool of [and a type of] the real Adversary, Satan.

This king of the North, is clearly identified as the system of the dragon, the scarlet beast, Satan (Rev 17); and as the final ruler of the Babylonian system of Daniel 2.

> **Revelation 12:3** And there appeared another wonder in heaven; and behold a **great red dragon** [Satan]**, having seven heads** [picturing the seven revivals of the Holy Roman Empire system] **and ten horns** [the final seventh revival consisting of ten rulers (nations) with a different man leading the whole system]**, and seven crowns** [one crown on each of its seven heads, representing the seven revivals of the Holy Roman Empire system] **upon his heads.**
>
> **12:4** And his tail **drew the third part of the stars** [angels] **of heaven, and did cast them to the earth** [the true dragon is Satan the devil, and the earthly Holy Roman Empire dragon system is of Satan the devil] **:** and the dragon stood before the woman which was ready to be delivered, for to devour her child as soon as it was born.

This final ruler called the king of the north [and the whole Babylonian Mysteries Holy Roman Empire system], will be destroyed by Jesus Christ at his coming, and Satan will also ultimately be destroyed by Christ as well.

Daniel 8:11 Yea, **he magnified himself even to** [against] **the prince of the host** [the high priest]**, and by him the daily sacrifice was taken away,** [this came in C 70 A.D. when the Roman prince Titus destroyed the temple at Jerusalem ending the sacrifices; which are not to resume until Christ comes and builds the Ezekiel temple.

. . . **and the place of the sanctuary was cast down** [this happened in c 70 A.D. and the city and people will again be taken in this latter day for the second half of the 70th week (Dan 9) or 42 months].

As Satan fights against God and tries to exalt himself above God; so this physical leader of the latter day kingdom of the north, will also seek to fight against the Word of God throughout his reign and at the coming of Christ. The physical end time ruler [the king of the North] shall occupy Jerusalem and the place of the sanctuary for 42 months (Rev 11:2).

This physical ruler is given an army to fight and overcome the people of God on the earth. Because of the great transgressions of the Ekklesia and the physical nations of Israel against the Word of God.

Power to make war will be given to this king of the North to overcome the called out, because of their many sins against the Eternal.

8:12 And **an host was given him against the daily sacrifice** [in c 70 A.D. Titus destroyed the Temple and stopped the Daily, and in this latter day the king of the North receives power for another 42 months, against physical and spiritual Israel, because of the multitude of our transgressions.] **by reason of transgression** [of the Ekklesia and the nations of Israel]**, and it cast down the truth to the ground; and it practised, and prospered.**

8:13 Then I heard one saint speaking, and another saint said unto that certain saint which spake, How long shall be the vision concerning [about when the daily will be cleansed] the daily sacrifice, and [when the abomination completes trampling the daily?] the transgression of desolation, to give both the sanctuary and the host to be trodden under foot?

The question here is about **how long the entire vision** of the king of the north is: NOT about how long the stopping of the daily will be!

The whole vision about the 2300 days, concerns the time from the fourth division of Alexander's empire being established and the first king of the North being set up, until Christ comes.

The 2,300 days is not about the daily sacrifice being stopped which was done by the Roman Prince Titus in c 70 A.D.; the 2,300 days is about the King of the North which began about 280 B.C, when Alexander's empire was finally divided into four parts.

The whole prophecy of the King of the North will last for 2,300 days [years]! Until the final king of the north is destroyed by Christ and the sanctuary is cleansed!

8:14 And he said unto me, **Unto two thousand and three hundred days; then shall the sanctuary be cleansed.**

Who comes to cleanse the sanctuary? Jesus Christ! Because Daniel 9 tells us that the sanctuary will lay desolate [will NOT be cleansed] until the consummation [completion] of the final 42 months of the second half of the full seven years.

Gabriel gives the interpretation of the vision.

8:15 And it came to pass, when I, even I Daniel, had seen the vision, and sought for the meaning, then, behold, there stood before me as the appearance of a man.

8:16 And I heard a man's voice between the banks of Ulai, which called, and said, Gabriel, make this man to understand the vision.

8:17 So he came near where I stood: and when he came, I was afraid, and fell upon my face: but he said unto me, Understand, O son of man: **for at the time of the end shall be the vision** [the cleansing of the sanctuary by the coming of Christ!].

8:18 Now as he was speaking with me, I was in a deep sleep [Daniel fainted and fell on his face] on my face toward the ground: but he touched me, and set me upright.

The vision covers the history of the King of the North from the division of Alexander's empire into four parts, up to the coming of Messiah the Christ; and Messiah's cleansing of the temple sanctuary!

8:19 And he said, Behold, I will make thee know what shall be in the last end of the indignation: for **at the time appointed** [at the end of the 2,300 days of the kingdom of the North.] **the end shall be**.

8:20 The ram which thou sawest having two horns are the kings of Media and Persia.

8:21 And the rough goat is the king of Grecia: and the great horn that is between his eyes is the first king.

8:22 Now that being broken, whereas four stood up for it, four kingdoms shall stand up out of the nation, but not in his power.

8:23 And **in the latter time of their kingdom**, when the transgressors are come to the full, a king of fierce countenance, and understanding dark sentences [The last king of the north shall understand secret things], shall stand up.

8:24 And his power shall be mighty, but not by his own power [by Satan's power]: and he shall destroy wonderfully [awesomely], and shall prosper, and practise, and shall destroy the mighty and the holy people.

He shall have power to overcome the Ekklesia and occupy Jerusalem and Judea for 42 months.

8:25 And through his policy also he shall cause craft to prosper in his hand; and he shall magnify himself in his heart [become very proud], and by peace shall destroy many: he shall also stand up against the Prince of princes; but he shall be broken without [this man and the entire system will be destroyed by Christ at his coming, without human hands] hand.

The vision that the sanctuary will be cleansed 2,300 days after the empire of Alexander is divided into four parts is true.

8:26 **And the vision of the evening and the morning which was told is true: wherefore shut thou up the vision; for it shall be for many days.**

8:27 And I Daniel fainted, and was sick certain days; afterward I rose up, and did the king's business; and I was astonished at the vision, but none understood it.

History

The sanctuary will be cleansed at the coming of Christ; therefore to have a good idea of when Christ will come, we must date the division of Alexander's empire into four parts and the beginning of the king of the North and then count forward 2,300 years; a day for a year.

The history of the successors of Alexander is very complex and extremely difficult, yet as we get closer and closer to the time; God is keeping his promise to Daniel and increasing knowledge and understanding day by day.

Historically, the first king of a united Greece was Alexander, who died in 323 B.C. after conquering the Medo-Persian Empire.

After his death, many men tried to assume his mantle as ruler of the lands that he had conquered.

In 304 B.C. Antigonus declared himself king and demanded that all the others submit to him. Cassander, Lysimachis, Nicator, Pyrrhus and Ptolemy did not agree and also declared themselves to be kings over their own lands.

In 301 B.C. Antigonus 1 was defeated and killed by the other five. Meanwhile, the son of Antigonus, Demetrius, was able to flee the field and continued as king of various areas in his father's place, thus keeping six kings.

In 297 B.C. Cassander died and was succeeded by his eldest son Philip, who in turn died the next year (296 B.C.). In 295 B.C., the widow of Cassander, Thessalonice; divided the kingdom of Macedonia between her two remaining sons, Antipater and Alexander. They took to quarreling and Antipater murdered his mother and attacked his brother Alexander. Alexander called for help from Demetrius, who came and murdered the young man, seizing his kingdom.

Demetrius then attacked Alexander's brother, Antipater, who fled to his uncle Lysimachis. Lysimachis had the lad executed for the murder of his sister, the boy's mother, in **294 B.C.** These events brought to an end the family of Cassander. Extinguishing Cassander, his wife and his three sons and **reducing the successors of Alexander to five; Demetrius, Ptolemy, Lysimachis, Pyrrhus and Seleucus Nicator.**

To further complicate things a number of the possessions of Demetrius declared their independence while these struggles were going on.

After Demetrius took the necessary time to secure Macedonia he proceeded to retake Thessaly and Boeotia in 291 B.C., completing the job in 290 BC.

Then in 288 B.C. Pyrrhus, Lysmachis and Ptolemy united against Demetrius and defeated him, making joint war against him and forcing him to abandon his kingdom of Macedonia.

Demetrius, left with only his possessions outside of Macedonia; tried to attack Seleucus and move into Asia with his army, but was finally taken prisoner in 285 BC after his army fell apart. His kingdom was then taken over by his son Antigonus 2 Gonatas

"In 285 B.C., Demetrius, worn down by his fruitless campaign, surrendered to Seleucus." In 283 B.C., at the age of 55, Demetrius died in captivity in Syria and was succeeded by his son Antigonus 2 Gonatas who continued to rule the kingdom of his father Demetrius.

Soon Lysimachus made the fatal mistake of having his son Agathocles murdered at the say-so of his second wife, Arsinoe (282 B.C.) who wanted her own son to become king.

The murdered Agathocles's widow, Lysandra, fled to Seleucus, who now made war upon Lysimachus.

Seleucus, after appointing his son Antiochus ruler of his Asian territories, defeated and killed Lysimachus at the Battle of Corupedium in Lydia in 281 B.C.; ending his kingdom. At this point the successors of Alexander still numbered five; with Antigonus, Ptolemy, Pyrrhus, Seleucus Nicator and Seleucus' son Antiochus [having been given some provinces as his own kingdom].

In 281 BC.. Seleucus was assassinated as he tried to invade Macedonia and Thrace.

Then certain Syrian officers of Seleucus rejected Antiochus from becoming their king in his father's place; seeking to take over the kingdom for themselves. Antiochus then invaded Syria from his own possessions to put down the pretenders to his father's throne, and became sole ruler of all his father's possessions in c 280 B.C.; fulfilling the prophecy that finally there would be only four divisions of Alexander's empire. Which four parts were established in 280 B.C. with Antigonus, Ptolemy, Pyrrhus and Antiochus.

I do want to caution that even though this looks and may be correct; we must still be alert to watch events and WAIT FOR THE SIGNS. This history is incredibly complex and there is the matter of the ancient Greek city state calendars as related to our common calendar today. **This could possibly be out by a few years.**

Nevertheless these things would be meaningless if we were to die tonight; it is imperative that we seek to be as close to God as possible. None of us is secure from sudden tragedy; therefore let us always put our trust in the only one who can save!

> **Ecclesiastes 12:13** Let us hear the conclusion of the whole matter: **Fear God, and keep his commandments: for this is the whole duty of man.**

The Vision is for The End Time

Daniel 8:17 For at the TIME of the END the VISION [The vision is about the end of the 2,300 days of years.] shall be

Daniel 8:19 Behold, I will make thee know what shall be in the LAST END of the indignation: for at the TIME APPOINTED the END SHALL BE.

Daniel 8:23 And in the LATTER TIME of their kingdom, when the transgressors are COME TO THE FULL,

This VISION, this prophecy, is for the END TIMES. This prophecy was not and could not, have been fulfilled by Antiochus Epiphanes over two thousand years ago!

The prophecy is for our day, NOW!

How long shall be the VISION?

Daniel 8:14 Unto 2300 days, then shall the sanctuary be cleansed.

Margin 2300 evenings and mornings. What is an evening and morning?

The evening and morning were the first day (Gen 1:5). The evening and morning were the second day (Gen 1:8). The evening and morning were the third day (Gen 1:13). One evening and one morning together are one day. Two evenings and mornings are two days. Three evenings and mornings are three days. One hundred evenings and mornings are one hundred days. **And, twenty-three hundred evenings and mornings are twenty-three hundred days!**

Suddenly from the four divisions of Alexander's kingdom and the founding of the king of the North in Daniel 8:8, the prophecy leaps forward to the last days and the cleansing of the sanctuary (Dan 8:9). Shown in the explanation; are the four divisions in verse twenty-two and then leaping forward to the LATTER TIME and the cleansing of the sanctuary in verse twenty-three.

In the LATTER TIME a fierce king shall appear, understanding secret [occult and highly technical matters] things and he shall destroy and prosper (Dan 8:23-24).

He shall destroy many while they are AT PEACE (Dan 8:25, 1 Thes 5:3).

He shall stand up against the Prince of Princes, Jesus Christ, at his coming (Dan 8:25), but he shall be broken (Dan 2:35) and thrown into the fire (Rev 19:20 and Dan 7:11).

This final fierce appearing king of the Babylonian system today rising up to be centered in Europe, and at its later end moving to Jerusalem; shall have power to make war, and to occupy Jerusalem; for forty two months or 1260 days (Rev 13:5); after which he and the false prophet will be destroyed and the sanctuary will be CLEANSED by the coming of Messiah the Christ who will build the Ezekiel Temple!

The whole vision about this competition between Babylon [the North] and Egypt/Judea [the South] is covered in Daniel 11.

The vision about Alexander's empire being divided into four parts, would last for **a total of 2300 days from the partition of Alexander's empire into four parts in c 280 BC**, and then [at the end of the 2,300 years] shall the sanctuary be cleansed (Dan 8:13-14).

The explanation is this:

From the time that Alexander's empire is divided into four parts, there will be 2300 days [years] until the sanctuary is cleansed and the destruction of the final seventh resurrection of the Holy Roman Empire of Babylon as described in Daniel 2 and Daniel 7.

At a day for a year this 2300 days is 2300 years in fulfillment.

Now subtracting 42 months (1260 days) we arrive in the winter of 2017 - 2018; **If the date beginning the count is correct.**

Given the historical difficulties of the Greek struggles **it is possible that this date might be in error by a few years,** but one thing is certain; IT IS VERY CLOSE INDEED!

These are indications of the nearness of the times only; they are not dates certain until proved by the appearance of ALL of the Biblical signs.

This man of sin will then go to the Holy Place [Temple Mount] 75 days after being set up in the Vatican and the great tribulation of Matthew 24:15 will begin.

Ezekiel 4

God commands Ezekiel to act out a siege of Jerusalem. If we also obey this command and act out this siege we will learn something more than we would by just reading the words. I ask each of you to act out this as Ezekiel was instructed to do, If you do not have a tile simply drawing on paper or using something in place of a tile for the city will still reveal the lesson.

Ezekiel 4:1 Thou also, son of man, take thee a tile, and lay it before thee, and pourtray upon it the city, even **Jerusalem: 4:2 And lay siege against it, and build a fort against it, and cast a mount against it; set the camp also against it, and set battering rams against it round about.**

We are to set up something representing Jerusalem, and then we are to besiege the city. Then we are to place an iron barrier between the city and the besiegers.

It should be immediately obvious that the city would be protected from the besiegers by the iron barrier between it and the besiegers.

4:3 Moreover take thou unto thee **an iron pan, and set it for a wall of iron between thee and the city: and set thy face against it, and it shall**

be besieged, and thou shalt lay siege against it. This shall be a sign to the house of Israel.

Then Ezekiel is told that he is to lie on his left side to bear the iniquity of Israel for 390 days and then to lay on his right side to bear the iniquity of Judah for 40 days; as a allegory of God bearing their iniquity for the same number of years.

To bear the iniquity of, means to put up with - to endure, to overlook - the sins of the people of Israel for 390 years, and the sins of the people of Judah for 40 years at a year for a day.

4:4 Lie thou also upon thy left side, and lay the iniquity of the house of Israel upon it: according to the number of the days that thou shalt lie upon it thou shalt bear their iniquity. **4:5** For **I have laid upon thee the years of their iniquity, according to the number of the days, three hundred and ninety days: so shalt thou bear the iniquity of the house of Israel.**

4:6 And when thou hast accomplished them, lie again on thy right side, and **thou shalt bear the iniquity of the house of Judah forty days:**

I have appointed thee each day for a year.

4:7 Therefore thou shalt set thy face toward the siege of Jerusalem, and thine arm shall be uncovered, and thou shalt prophesy against it. **4:8** And, behold, I will lay bands upon thee, and thou shalt not turn thee from one side to another, **till thou hast ended the days of thy siege.**

The city of Jerusalem being besieged, but with an iron barrier protecting the city; represents today's Jewish state being under God's blessing and protection for 40 years and represents the ten tribes of Israel [mainly the Anglo Saxon people] being under God's blessing and protection for 390 years in the latter days. Then when God's protection and blessing are completed, Israel and Judah will fall together.

We know from Hosea 5:5 that in the end time BOTH Israel and Judah will fall together.

Hosea 5:5 And the pride of Israel doth testify to his face: therefore shall Israel and Ephraim fall in their iniquity: Judah also shall fall with them.

Ezekiel was only one man and he could not lie on both sides at once, but it is clear that BOTH periods of years end at the same time; and that BOTH Israel and Judah shall fall together which has never happened before in history.

This strange exercise means that in the end times will bless and protect Israel [mainly the Anglo Saxon peoples] and today's Jewish state for these set numbers of years, to fulfil the promises made to Abraham, and the prophecies of the end times blessings of Jacob [Israel] might be fulfilled (Gen 49, Deu 33)!

These periods of years picture Israel [mainly the Anglo Saxon peoples] and today's Jewish state as being vexed by enemies but blessed with the blessing of strong protection from God; God fulfilling his promises to our ancestors regarding the blessing on our people for the last days so that the promises of God are not broken!

In October 1978 a peace treaty was agreed between Egypt and the Jewish state with the United States [the Anglo Saxon peoples of America being one of the ten tribes of Israel] guaranteeing the security of the modern Jewish state against all enemies. The treaty was actually signed on 26 March 1979, and became effective January 1980. IF this peace treaty is what is meant by the 40 year prophecy then the tribulation could begin in either late 2019 or 2020 depending on the date used; either the signing date or the effective date.

Exactly how long after the end of God's protection before the tribulation begins remains to be seen, but it would seem to be less than one year otherwise the prophecy would say 41 years instead of 40 years.

Once the miracle working Roman Pontiff visits the Holy Mount (Mat 24:15) the Tribulation will begin with the occupation of Jerusalem for 42 months Rev 11:2).

Now comes a complication that has confused people through the generations. People have naturally assumed that the following famine takes place during the time of the "siege:" which it does NOT!

It is AFTER the siege when God's protection and blessing has ended; that the Eternal will send Israel [mainly the Anglo Saxon peoples] and today's Jewish state into a final affliction. It is after the siege is over and the iron plate of the heavenly protection and blessing for Israel [mainly the Anglo Saxon peoples] and todays Jewish state HAS BEEN STOPPED; that Israel [mainly the Anglo Saxon peoples] and today's Jewish state will go into a period of affliction and will experience great famine!

Remember that it is when the siege [God's protection which keeps Israel and Judah from falling] ends [v 13] and the city falls, that Israel [mainly the Anglo Saxon peoples] and today's Jewish state will fall into severe affliction.

Once Jerusalem and Judea are occupied the people of Judah will be placed into ghettos, where they will suffer greatly. Many will die and many others will be deported from Palestine. At the same time Turkey and the Arab countries will reject the Petrodollar and join in alliance with the New Federal Europe, with the rest of the world following suit and also rejecting the Petrodollar. This will send America and dollar dependent Anglo Saxon countries like Canada and Britain into financial collapse and subsequent severe suffering including famine, disease and internal violence.

Ezekiel 4:9 Take thou also unto thee wheat, and barley, and beans, and lentiles, and millet, and fitches, and put them in one vessel, and make thee bread thereof, according to the number of the days that thou shalt lie upon thy side, three hundred and ninety days shalt thou eat thereof. **4:10** And thy meat which thou shalt eat shall be by weight, twenty shekels a day: from time to time shalt thou eat it.

4:11 Thou shalt drink also water by measure, the sixth part of an hin [about a pint] : from time to time shalt thou drink. **4:12** And thou shalt eat it as barley cakes, and thou shalt bake it with dung that cometh out of man, in their sight.

This famine will fall on Israel and Judah after God's blessings and protection ends, pictured by a stopping of the spiritual Daily Sacrifice; which is the intercession of the spiritual High Priest, Jesus Christ in heaven!

The siege is all about God's IRON protection to give to them Israel [mainly the Anglo Saxon peoples] and today's Jewish state the promised end times blessings of God!

The end of the siege pictures the stopping of the heavenly spiritual Daily Sacrifice and God's blessings because of our many great sins, and then the sending forth of the people into a final affliction called the great tribulation for 42 months (Rev 11:2).

It is at the end of the period of the end times blessings of 390 years for Israel [Britain and America] and the 40 years protection for the modern Jewish state; the intercession, blessing and protection of God will be stopped because of our wickedness and the people will go forth into great tribulation including severe famine.

4:13 And the LORD said, Even thus shall the children of Israel eat their defiled bread among the Gentiles, **whither I will drive them** [after the siege ends and the city is taken].

Ezekiel protests to YHVH that he would not eat anything unclean. Do you get that; here Ezekiel is protesting to the Eternal that he would not violate the law of God even at God's command! Centuries later Peter would do the same thing in Acts 10!

Was God testing Ezekiel as to his zeal for the Word of God? Nearly all of us have disgracefully failed similar tests such as the temptation to buy in restaurants on Sabbath and Holy Days!

The unclean food was to represent that Israel [mainly the Anglo Saxon peoples] and today's Jewish state would be forced to eat all manner of filth just to survive in the last 42 months before Messiah comes; after making that point the Eternal allows Ezekiel an alternative so that Ezekiel could keep God's Word.

4:14 Then said I, Ah Lord GOD! behold, my soul hath not been polluted: for from my youth up even till now have I not eaten of that which dieth of itself, or is torn in pieces; neither came there abominable flesh into my mouth. **4:15** Then he said unto me, Lo, I have given thee cow's dung for man's dung, and thou shalt prepare thy bread therewith.

Then God makes a prophecy of famine specific to Jerusalem and this will spread from Jerusalem [as the capital city representing the whole nation] to other places during the tribulation.

4:16 Moreover he said unto me, Son of man, behold, I will break the staff of bread in Jerusalem: and they shall eat bread by weight, and with care; and they shall drink water by measure, and with astonishment [water will be very scarce and must not be wasted]: **4:17** That they may want bread and water, and be astonied one with another, and consume away for their iniquity.

Dating the Coming of Messiah

The Daniel 8 study on the 2,300 Day prophecy reveals that Messiah the Christ would come to cleanse the sanctuary and build the Ezekiel Temple 2,300 years [at a day for a year] after the empire of Alexander was divided into four parts. That happened in approximately 280 B.C. and counting forward 2,300 years brings the coming of Christ in early 2022.

The problem with this date is the word "approximately," because in fact pin pointing the precise date that Alexander's empire was divided into four parts is impossible and with the start of the count not precisely known, any count could be in error by a year or more. Therefore the coming of Christ in early 2022 is only a general, vague, ball park date, and is not a set in stone firm precise date. it is an approximation only.

We must now look for confirmation of the Daniel 8 2300 day prophecy in Holy Scripture and we find it in the Ezekiel 4 - 5 forty year prophecy.

God reveals to Ezekiel that in the latter days he would protect the Jewish state for forty years before giving her over to severe correction. we all know that independence came in 1948 which is much longer than forty years ago so what does this forty years of protection mean?

In October 1978 a peace treaty was agreed between Egypt and the Jewish state with the United States [the Anglo Saxon peoples of America being one of the ten tribes of Israel] guaranteeing the security of the modern Jewish state against all enemies.

The treaty was actually signed on 26 March 1979, and became effective January 1980. IF this peace treaty is what is meant by the 40 year prophecy, then the tribulation could begin in either late 2018, 2019 or 2020 depending on the date used; either the agreement, or the signing date or the effective date.

Daniel 9 tells us that this tribulation or Time of Jacob's trouble will last for 42 months; if we add forty years plus 42 months for the tribulation to the peace treaty between the Jewish state and Egypt we arrive at 2022, 2023 or 2024 for the coming of Christ.

After the dust has settled from the looming Mideast regional war and new governments are in place, Trump is to release his peace plan which will be a call to a genuine dialogue for peace guided by a list of parameters put together by the Trump team.

The peace talks could then take months to reach an agreement. Together with the regional war it could easily take another year or more [from today] for a peace deal to be concluded.

This leaves us with very little time before a peace is achieved and the 42 month tribulation begins, then Messiah the Christ will come to save humanity from self-destruction 42 months after the tribulation begins.

Daniel 9: The 70 Weeks Prophecy

The Second Half of the 70th Week

There are those who believe that the full 70th week of Daniel 9 is still to come with a period of 3 1/2 years after a peace deal in the Middle East before the tribulation begins.

There are a variety of explanations concerning the Seventieth or Last Week, of the Seventy Weeks Prophecy. Most of which have been around for a long time and were first put forth as a part of the Protestant Reformation. We know that these explanations cannot be true because the understanding of these things has been sealed until the last days.

Daniel 12:9 And he said, Go thy way, Daniel: for **the words are closed up and sealed till the time of the end.**

A common explanation of the seventieth week put out by certain Groups, is that the False Prophet will make a peace deal with Judah, possibly allowing them to build a Temple or set up a Tabernacle and start sacrifices.

Then after 3 1/2 years; the peace covenant will be broken, the sacrifices stopped and the tribulation will begin and last for a second 3 1/2 years. This explanation gives rise to the theory that a Temple, or at least some kind of Tabernacle must be built and physical sacrifices must start.

We KNOW that this explanation CANNOT BE TRUE for the scripture says that when "Peace and Safety" is declared; SUDDEN, IMMEDIATE, AT THAT TIME; destruction will come: 1 Thes 5:3. There will be NO 3 1/2 years of peace!

Jesus Christ said that when the abomination spoken of by Daniel goes to the Holy Place; sudden, immediate great tribulation will begin (Mat 24:15).

Daniel tells us that his prophetic words are SEALED UNTIL THE END (Dan 12:9). This means that explanations written many years ago: CANNOT BE CORRECT.

The seventieth week of the prophecy is found in Daniel 9:24-27.

Each week is seven days; so seven weeks is forty nine days and sixty two weeks is four hundred and thirty four days.

Each day representing one year, therefore the city would be built in forty nine years, then Messiah would come after another four hundred and thirty four years. Indicating that Messiah would come four hundred and eighty three years after the commandment to rebuild the city was issued.

Then at an unspecified point after the four hundred and eighty three years, Messiah shall be cut off, but not for Himself: and then after Christ's death, resurrection and ascension, came the fist half of the 70th week when the Ekklesia fled to Pella and the first century destruction of Jerusalem and the temple by Titus stopped the daily sacrifice after a 42 month siege.

Daniel 9:24 Seventy weeks are determined upon thy people and upon thy holy city, to FINISH TRANSGRESSION, and to make an END OF SINS, and to make RECONCILIATION FOR INIQUITY, and to BRING IN EVERLASTING RIGHTEOUSNESS, and to SEAL UP THE VISION AND PROPHESY, and to ANOINT THE MOST HOLY .

In the first century reconciliation was offered to only a very few and transgressions have not yet been finished on this earth, nor yet in Judah, nor has sin been ended. It is when He shall return that Messiah shall be Anointed King over all the earth and will put an end to all wickedness.

Titus and the first Roman destruction of Jerusalem ending the Daily

Daniel 9:25 And the people of the prince that shall come shall destroy the city and the sanctuary: and the end thereof shall be with a flood, and unto the end of the war desolations are determined.

And He [Messiah] shall CONFIRM A COVENANT [the New Covenant] for one week [seven years]:

The prophecy now addresses the siege of Jerusalem by Prince Titus

. . . and in the midst of the week [at the end of the first 3 1/2 years, after a 42 month siege during which the Ekklesia had fled to Pella]; He [The Roman Prince Titus besieged Jerusalem and after 42 months the city fell and the temple was burned stopping the daily sacrifice.] shall cause the sacrifice and oblation to cease and for the overspreading of abominations He shall make it desolate [This was fulfilled at the end of the first half of the week when God allowed Prince Titus to destroy the temple.], even until the consummation [The temple will remain destroyed and the daily sacrifice stopped until the end of the age and the completion of the seventy weeks, when Christ comes to build the Ezekiel Temple!], and that determined shall be poured upon the desolator [the final abomination will be destroyed at the coming of Messiah, Daniel 9:27].

At that time, the New Covenant of espousal between Jesus Christ and the called out was confirmed for the first half of the 70th week when the Ekklesia fled to Pella about c 66 A.D., to be preserved from the destruction of the Roman war against Jerusalem! This fulfilled the first 3 1/2 years or the first half of the 70th week, as I shall presently show!

Once the Romans had destroyed the temple and ended the Daily Sacrifice; at the END of three and a half years of war [in the midst of the week]; it is prophesied that **the temple will not be rebuilt, and that the Daily Sacrifice will not be renewed and not resume; until the end of the second half of the week and the coming of Messiah:** Until the consummation, or end, of the 70 weeks!

The time line of The Seventy Weeks Prophecy

1) The decree goes out to build the city; Messiah appears and begins his ministry in autumn 27 A.D. 483 years after the command to rebuild the city,

He is cut off 3 1/2 years later and resurrected; only then does the New Covenant officially begin, and verse 27,

2) Jesus Christ confirms the New Covenant with many by taking them and preserving them in Pella during the 42 month siege of Jerusalem for the first half of a week or 3 1/2 years, fulfilled in years for days!

3) Then after a 3 1/2 year siege, at the end of the first half of the seventieth week and before the second half of the seventieth week, God caused the sacrifice and oblation to cease by allowing Prince Titus to conquer Jerusalem and destroy the city and the temple; stopping the daily sacrifice!

Brethren, the physical daily sacrifice has already been stopped and it is to remain stopped until the consummation of the end of the 70th week and the coming of Christ!

NOTICE: The seventieth week does NOT BEGIN until after the resurrection of Jesus Christ. It is not until c 66 A.D. that the first half of the seventieth week is confirmed for three and one half years by the protection of the faithful in Pella during the siege of Jerusalem by the Romans; and it is not until our day that the second half of the 70th week will come, as per Daniel 9.

What covenant is being talked about?

Why, the New Covenant which was not made sure until after the sacrifice of Christ was accepted by the Father on Wave Offering Sunday. The MARRIAGE Covenant of Espousal, of Betrothal; between Jesus Christ and His called out first fruits, His bride; was then made official at Pentecost 31 A.D.

Jesus Christ the espoused Husband, promised to nurture and care for and to protect the bride; and the espoused bride [the sincerely repentant] promises to love, be faithful to and to fully obey Him.

The New Covenant like the Mosaic Covenant is a Marriage Covenant!

Christ would then confirm His New Covenant with His espoused bride when the city (Jerusalem) was under siege and destroyed in circa 70 A.D. (Dan 9:26-27).

In the first century, the faithful fled to Pella in Jordan and remained there for the first 1/2 week (a day for a year; 3 1/2 years) preserved by Jesus Christ from the Roman armies, in a first century fore-type of the final 42 month great tribulation.

This refuge in Pella for 1,260 days, fulfilled the first half of the 70th week

The people of the prince that shall come shall destroy the city and the sanctuary; and the end thereof shall be with a flood, and unto the end of the war desolations are determined (Dan 9:26).

Messiah had no sin and did not die for His own sin, but died for the sins of mankind. AFTER His death and resurrection, Judah rebelled against Rome and was destroyed, Jerusalem falling in c 70 AD. This was a precursor of or a fore-type of; the final great tribulation.

And He [Christ] shall CONFIRM A COVENANT for one week: and in the midst of the week He [Christ] shall cause the sacrifice and oblation to cease and for the overspreading of abominations [Christ shall give the city over to a desolator, the Roman prince Titus; and this will be repeated in the last days with the second half of the week (3 1/2 years)].

The Roman prince Titus made the Temple and the Daily Sacrifice desolate, and it will remain desolate, even until the consummation [the end of the 70th week and the coming of Messiah, and that determined [When the King of kings comes he will destroy the desolating political leader and his false prophet with their armies.] shall be poured upon the desolator (Dan 9:27).

Notice the time-line. The seventieth week, of seven years; does not begin until after the death and resurrection of Christ!

Jesus Christ was to appear at the end of the seven plus sixty-two weeks (69 weeks) Dan 9:26, which was in 27 A.D.

There is no way that the ministry of Christ could have fulfilled the first half of the 70th week since this could ONLY be fulfilled AFTER he was "Cut Off," AFTER he was killed and resurrected!

The first half or the 70th week was fulfilled when the faithful fled Jerusalem for Pella in c 66 A.D.

According to the time line and the flow of events, the 70th week could not begin until Messiah had been "Cut Off" and resurrected, rising to be accepted by the Father on Wave Offering Sunday for us.

ONLY when Christ was accepted as our sacrifice and High Priest, could there be a Covenant to confirm; for the Mosaic Covenant was ended by his death as Husband of Israel, and the New Covenant did not officially begin until Christ was accepted by the Father.

Then He, Jesus Christ, PERSONALLY; not some apostle or disciple, shall confirm a covenant for seven years, or one prophetic week after His resurrection.

The New Covenant could NOT OFFICIALLY BEGIN until Jesus Christ fulfilled His mission and died to pay the penalty for the sins of men. Therefore only after Messiah had died and been resurrected could the New Covenant be confirmed.

ONLY AFTER THE DEATH AND SACRIFICE OF JESUS CHRIST COULD THE NEW COVENANT BE CONFIRMED; the first half of the last seventieth week could not begin until after the death and resurrection of Christ!

Therefore Messiah could not have been confirming a part of the 70th week covenant during His physical earthly ministry; as some wrongly teach.

In the midst of the week, after three and one half years of siege and before the final three and one half years; God caused the daily sacrifice to be stopped by allowing Prince Titus to destroy the temple in c 70 A.D.

As Jerusalem will once again be given over to her enemies (Rev 11:2, Rev 12:6), Jesus Christ will protect the faithful bride once again, for 1/2 week (3 1/2 years) thus confirming the New Covenant of ESPOUSAL with His Bride for the second half of the 70th week.

What covenant is being confirmed? The ONLY covenant mentioned in scripture to exist after the resurrection of Christ; THE NEW COVENANT, between Christ and those called out of season as a kind of first fruits of the NEW COVENANT of Jeremiah 31:31!

What does confirmed mean? To fulfill, to make sure. What is this covenant? A marriage agreement to PROTECT, NOURISH and CARE FOR His espoused bride, those who KEEP HIS COMMANDMENTS!

PROOF: The true explanation of the whole 70th Week is found in Revelation 12.

> **Revelation 12:1** And there appeared a great wonder in heaven; a woman clothed with the sun, and the moon under her feet, and upon her head a crown of twelve stars: **12:2** And she being with child cried, travailing in birth, and pained to be delivered.

This speaks of the mother of Christ, as a type of the called out faithful Ekklesia.

> **12:3** And there appeared another wonder in heaven; and behold a great red dragon, having seven heads and ten horns, and seven crowns upon his heads.

This is Satan, and later Satan's system on the earth is described as the scarlet beast; Scarlet being red. This is explained in Revelation 17 which will be included in a future book.

> **12:4** And his tail drew the third part of the stars of heaven, and did cast them to the earth: and the dragon stood before the woman which was ready to be delivered, for to devour her child as soon as it was born.

Satan at his original fall, led a third of the angels with him, and as the Christ was ready to be born, he stood up to destroy him.

> **12:5** And she brought forth a man child, who was to rule all nations with a rod of iron: and her child was caught up unto God, and to his throne.

The child being spoken of, is identified as Christ the Messiah; for ONLY Christ has died and been resurrected to spirit and ascended to the Father's throne.

Now we come to the first half of the 70th week; the first 3 1/2 year flight of the faithful, which was to Pella; NOT Petra!

> **12:6** And the woman fled into the wilderness, where she hath a place prepared of God, that they should feed her there a thousand two hundred and threescore days.

This was the first one half of the 70 Weeks, for 1,260 days, which is 42 months, or one half of seven years. The 70th Week, being 7 years, or 2520 days.

The first 3 1/2 years were fulfilled when the saints fled from Jerusalem to Pella, when the Romans besieged Jerusalem.

Now NOTICE that; at an unspecified time [in this prophecy; but actually specified in the 2,300 day prophecy] AFTER that; there was war in heaven. This is clearly at the end time, for it begins after the first half, and before the second half of the week.

12:7 And there was war in heaven: Michael and his angels fought against the dragon; and the dragon fought and his angels, [This is AFTER the first half of the week has passed, and just before the second half of the 70th week begins.]

12:8 And prevailed not; neither was their place found any more in heaven. 12:9 And the great dragon was cast out, that old serpent, called the Devil, and Satan, which deceiveth the whole world: he was cast out into the earth, and his angels were cast out with him.

Daniel 12:1 tells us that Michael shall stand up to fight against Satan and cast him to the earth, which will be right before the beginning of the tribulation.

Daniel 12:1 And at that time shall Michael stand up, the great prince which standeth for the children of thy people: **and there shall be a time of trouble, such as never was since there was a nation even to that same time:** and at that time thy people shall be delivered [Rescued by the coming of Messiah!], every one that shall be found written in the book.

Just before the onset of the latter 42 month tribulation, Satan rises up to fight against God, knowing that his imprisonment is at hand, and is defeated and thrown down

Revelation 12:10 And I heard a loud voice saying in heaven, Now is come salvation, and strength, and the kingdom of our God, and the power of his Christ: for the accuser of our brethren is cast down, which accused them before our God day and night.

12:11 And they overcame him by the blood of the Lamb, and by the word of their testimony; and they loved not their lives unto the death [they died for godliness].

12:12 Therefore rejoice, ye heavens, and ye that dwell in them. Woe to the inhabiters of the earth and of the sea! for the devil is come down unto you, having great wrath, because he knoweth that he hath but a short time [That is 3 1/2 years remaining to him].

All converted faithful believers are to rejoice and to hold their heads up high, as they see the imminence of the resurrection to eternal life and the Marriage to the Lamb of God!

The sinful need fear great sorrows because they must go through great tribulation for their sins.

12:13 And when the dragon saw that he was cast unto the earth, he persecuted the woman which brought forth the man child.

Obviously Mary could not have lived into the end time; therefore the woman is the body of the faithful believers and doers of the will of God.

Satan through his human instruments works to destroy all who will not bow to him. This is fully empowered by the setting up of the Abomination in Rome, the setting up of the New Europe and the Beast Emperor and the subsequent wars. This will be discussed in future volumes.

This miracle working abomination [false prophet, son of perdition.] will then go to the Holy Place to trigger the war within 75 days AFTER he is set up in Rome. Just before the second half of the seventieth week [just before the final 42 months] the woman [the Ekklesia] flees to Pella for the second time!

12:14 And to the woman were given two wings of a great eagle, that she might fly into the wilderness, into her place, where she is nourished for a time, and times, and half a time, from the face of the serpent.

The time, times and half a time are 3 1/2 years or 1,260 days, or 42 months; the second half of the 70th Week!

The "Great Eagle" is God, to whom the saints are faithful; and the two wings that are given to the saints that remove them to the place prepared: Are the Two Prophets of Zechariah 4 and Revelation 11, sent by God!

12:15 And the serpent cast out of his mouth water as a flood after the woman, that he might cause her to be carried away of the flood.

12:16 And the earth helped the woman, and the earth opened her mouth, and swallowed up the flood which the dragon cast out of his mouth.

When the faithful arrive in Moab in the near future, Satan will inspire an army to chase and attack the Ekklesia, as Jordan will be allied with the New Europe and Beast Emperor, Psalm 83.

The flood is a flood of men, a pursuing army; and God will cause an earthquake to destroy them.

Then Satan will turn back to attack the majority of the Ekklesia who have initially not believed the warnings, but who after this tribulation begins, will then remember and believe and bitterly sincerely repent.

12:17 And the dragon was wroth with the woman, and went to make war with the remnant of her seed, which keep the commandments of God, and have the testimony of Jesus Christ.

At the moment that the faithful escape, Satan will turn to destroy the Israelite nations and those who make a show of keeping the commandments; while being lukewarm for the things of God and idolizing those organizations and false prophets who have convinced them to ignore and reject the warnings from God through his servants and in particular the warnings from God's Two Prophets.

Jesus Christ will protect and nourish his people who are faithful to him! He did this for the first half of the 70th week during the siege of Jerusalem after his resurrection; and he will do this for second half of the 70th week at this end time!

The two halves complete one full week; the 70th Week of the prophecy!

Remember that one half of a week is three and one half days, which is three and one half years [at a day for a year] or forty two months or 1260 days. The explanation is found in the twelfth chapter of Revelation!

A woman clothed with the sun (the brightness of the LIGHT), and the moon under her feet (the power of the night, darkness) and wearing a crown of twelve stars (a Queen) brought forth a man child who was to rule all nations (Jesus Christ).

She fled into the wilderness where she was fed (nourished) by God for 1260 days [1/2 week =42 months = 3 1/2 days = 3 1/2 years = 1,260 days].

Later there was war in heaven and Satan was cast out (triggering a great time of trouble in the later days Dan 12:1) and he went to persecute that same woman, who again fled, INTO HER PLACE, where she is again nourished for a time, times and half a time; the times of the Gentiles Daniel 12:7, or 1260 days.

The woman is symbolic of the faithful who KEEP THE COMMANDMENTS of God, HAVING THE LAW OF GOD WRITTEN IN THEIR HEARTS (Heb 8:10). And the nourishing for these two halves of the week; is the confirming of the husband's part of the New Covenant by Jesus Christ!

This was just before the city was destroyed in the Jewish-Roman wars. See: Josephus, Wars of the Jews, the fall of Jerusalem. The city was surrounded in c 66 A.D. and then Vespasian was recalled to Rome after the suicide of Nero. the siege was slightly relaxed and a voice was heard in the temple declaring: "let us remove hence." The faithful then fled to Pella in what is now Jordan.

Then Vespasian on becoming emperor sent his son, Prince Titus to continue the war. Titus himself later became emperor in 79 A.D.

The Daily Sacrifice was offered on behalf of the entire nation and represents the bearing of the national sins of the entire nation! The physical daily was stopped by God at the END of the first 41 months through the instrument of Prince Titus!

Seek the LORD with all your hearts; Turn to a zeal for God to learn and to keep his Word; and he will deliver us, for those who love God enough to learn and to keep his Word are his precious jewels.

The Eternal is a RIGHTEOUS GOD, who KEEPS HIS COVENANTS; He will fulfill His role as a loving husband to a faithful wife.

Yes Jesus Christ loves his bride as only he can love therefore, FEAR NOT and HOLD YOUR HEADS UP, YOU WHO LOVE YOUR GOD AND DO HIS WILL Luk 21:28 FOR YOUR REDEMPTION DRAWS NEAR.

Be strong and of a good courage to follow the Mighty One who inhabits eternity!

These two periods of 3 1/2 years each, total the seven years of the last 70th week of the prophecy.

Yes; He, Jesus Christ will confirm His New Marriage Covenant with His loyal faithful espoused Bride for a full week!

1. The first half of the 70th week was fulfilled in the first century when the Ekklesia fled to Pella as the Romans besieged Jerusalem for 42 months, stopping the daily at the end of that 42 months.

2. The temple and the daily sacrifice will remain desolate until Messiah comes to build the Ezekiel Temple.

3. The second half of the 70th week will begin with the taking of Jerusalem in the latter days (Rev 13:5, Rev 11:2, Luk 21:24 and Rev

12:6), and Jesus Christ will take his faithful espoused bride to the place which God has prepared and nourish her there for 42 months: The second time!

When ALL the Biblical signs are present; when the final false prophet goes to the Holy Mount, as Peace and Safety is being declared: sudden destruction will come upon a stubborn and rebellious people (Mat 24:14, 1 Thess 5:3).

Many lukewarm people in the faith, who have lost their zeal for living by every Word of God, and fallen into a lukewarm complacency, will lack the oil of God's Spirit to respond to the warnings; and will become the victims of a strong delusion: Preferring to lean on their own false traditions and looking to idols of corporate organizations and men, instead of standing on the Word of God; they will fall into the correction of great tribulation.

Appendix 1

Biblical Nations Identified

After the great flood it did not take long for the descendants of Noah to turn away from God. At that time most people began to follow a man instead of God and God divided the families of man into today's racial linguistic groups.

> **Genesis 11:6** And the LORD said, Behold, the people is one, and they have all one language; and this they begin to do: and now nothing will be restrained from them, which they have imagined to do.
>
> **11:7** Go to, let us go down, and there confound their language, that they may not understand one another's speech.
>
> **11:8** So the LORD scattered them abroad from thence upon the face of all the earth: and they left off to build the city.
>
> **11:9** Therefore is the name of it called Babel; because the LORD did there confound the language of all the earth: and from thence did the LORD scatter them abroad upon the face of all the earth.

The three sons of Noah were Shem, Ham and Japhath and God divided their descendants by their families and scattered them to the corners of the earth.

The main families of mankind spread out from Babel [Babylon].

Genesis 10:1 Now these are the generations of the sons of Noah, Shem, Ham, and Japheth: and unto them were sons born after the flood.

The Descendants of Japheth

Genesis 10:2 The sons of Japheth;

Gomer, and Magog, and Madai, and Javan, and Tubal, and Meshech, and Tiras.

10:3 And the sons of Gomer;

Ashkenaz, and Riphath, and Togarmah.

10:4 And the sons of Javan;

Elishah, and Tarshish, Kittim, and Dodanim.

10:5 By these were the isles of the Gentiles divided in their lands; every one after his tongue, after their families, in their nations.

The Family of Gomer;

Ashkenaz: The modern Armenians

Togormah: Modern Georgia

Riphath: The Azeri people of modern Azerbaijan

The Family of Magog:

The peoples of modern central Asia

The Family of Madai:

Became the Medes of the Medo-Persian Empire and after the fall of that empire migrated into eastern Europe where they are known today as the Ukrainians and other closely related peoples.

The Family of Javan:

Elishah: Modern Greek Cyprus

Tarshish: Identified with Tartessus; Spain and Portugal

Kittim: Crete

Dodanim: The people of the Isle of Rhodes

The Family of Tubal:

Generally the Slavic peoples of the Balkans

The Family of Meshech:

Became modern Russia [Rosh]. Moscow (*Moskva*) was founded by King Mosokh son of Japheth (i.e. Meshech), and was named for him.

The Descendants of Ham

Genesis 10:6 And the sons of Ham; Cush, and Mizraim, and Phut, and Canaan.

As with Peleg no descendants of Phut are mentioned here, probably meaning that Phut remained as one united family. Yet Phut had descendants because soldiers of Phut are mentioned as serving Tyre in Ezekiel 27:10

10:7 And **the sons of Cush**;

Seba, and Havilah, and Sabtah, and Raamah, and Sabtechah: and the sons of Raamah; Sheba, and Dedan. [and Nimrod also]

10:8 And **Cush begat Nimrod**: he began to be a mighty one in the earth.

10:9 He was a mighty hunter before [in place of, or supplanting the LORD to lead men after himself] the LORD: wherefore it is said, Even as Nimrod the mighty hunter before the LORD.

10:10 And the beginning of his kingdom was Babel, and Erech, and Accad, and Calneh, in the land of Shinar.

The Family of Cush:

Seba, Havilah: Ethiopia and black Africa

Sabtah, Raamah and Sabtechah: Are the darker peoples of modern India

An Inset regarding Asshur son of Shem

Genesis 10:11 Out of that land [Babel] went forth Asshur, and builded Nineveh, and the city Rehoboth, and Calah,

10:12 And Resen between Nineveh and Calah: the same is a great city.

10:13 And Mizraim begat

Ludim, and Anamim, and Lehabim, and Naphtuhim,

10:14 And Pathrusim, and Casluhim, (out of whom came Philistim [modern Gazans],) and Caphtorim.

.

The Family of Mizraim [Hebrew Mizraim; Greek AEgyptos]

Ludim: Their land was to the far west of Libya in Algeria, Tunisia, Morocco, North Africa along the Mediterranean Sea

Anamim: The Bible generally refers to the Egyptians as Mizraim, many ancient peoples referred to the Egyptians as "*Anami*"

Lehabim: Eastern Libya along the Egyptian border

Naphtuhim: Migrated from Memphis to South Egypt

Pathrusim: Lived at Pathros in Upper Egypt

Casluhim: Settled on the sea coast between Sinai and Ashkelon. They are the modern people of Gaza, the ancient Philistines. The people of Gaza are not the same people as the Palestinians.

Caphtorim: an Egyptian coastal locality in the vicinity of Pelusium

The Family of Canaan

Sidon remains Sidon of modern Lebanon

10:15 And **Canaan begat** Sidon [who founded today's Sidon, Lebanon] his first born, and Heth,

The Hittites [Franks]

Heth the second son of Canaan was the father of the Hittites [later called Franks by the Romans] most of whom eventually migrated to Asia Minor, finally founding an empire with the capitol city of Troy.

WIKI: "The Trojan War was waged against the city of Troy by the Achaeans (Greeks) after Paris king of Troy took Helen from her husband Menelaus, king of Sparta."

After their empire was defeated and the Hittites [called Franks by the Romans] were expelled from Troy they migrated to northern Europe where they set up the empire of the Franks from which the word "France" is derived.

Although the Franks lived in northern France, today the whole nation of France is named after the Franks and the capitol of France still bears the name of the Hittite king of Troy "Paris."

Genesis 10:16 And the Jebusite, and the Amorite, and the Girgasite,

10:17 And the Hivite, and the Arkite, and the Sinite,

10:18 And the Arvadite, and the Zemarite, and the Hamathite: and **afterward were the families of the Canaanites spread abroad.**

After Israel entered the land of Canaan many Canaanites were destroyed, some remained and many others migrated from the area.

10:19 And the border of the Canaanites was from Sidon, as thou comest to Gerar, unto Gaza; as thou goest, unto Sodom, and Gomorrah, and Admah, and Zeboim, even unto Lasha.

The families of Canaan formed the Canaanite tribes bordered on the west by Gaza, Sidon and the sea, and including Sodom on the east.

Judges 2:2 describes God's message to sinning Israel. "you have not obeyed my voice, why have you done this?" Israel's punishment is found in Judges 2:21, "I will not henceforth drive out from before them any of the nations which Joshua left when he died." And that specifically was the Gaza Strip the area of Philistia, and the Canaanites in Lebanon.

The first verses of Judges 3 detail the peoples who would remain. "Now these are the nations which the Lord left, to prove Israel by them, even as many of Israel as had not known all the wars of Canaan. Namely, five lords of the Philistines [the Philistines are Not Canaanites], and all the Canaanites, and the Sidonians, and the Hivites that dwelt in **mount Lebanon, from mount Baalhermon** [Mount Hermon] **unto the entering in of Hamath."** .

Others like the Hittites also remained in the land for a time. Heth the second son of Canaan was the father of the Hittites [later called Franks by the Romans]. The Hittites lived in Hebron (Gen 23:18-20) until most of whom were driven out of Canaan by Nebuchadnezzar and eventually migrated to Asia Minor, finally founding an empire with the capital city of Troy.

Later God removed the ten tribes from Samaria and gave the land north of Jerusalem to a people from Mesopotamia (2 Kings 17:24), who began to be called Samaritans by the Jews since their main center was in Samaria.

Today the native Canaanite tribes remain in Lebanon, and have been spread widely abroad; but the bulk of the Palestinians are descendants of the Samaritans now converted to Islam or Catholicism.

10:20 These are the sons of Ham, after their families, after their tongues, in their countries, and in their nations.

The Descendants of Shem

Genesis 10:21 Unto Shem also, the father of all the children of Eber, the brother of Japheth the elder [his elder brother, both being the sons of Noah], even to him were children born.

10:22 The children of Shem;

Elam, and Asshur, and Arphaxad, and Lud, and Aram.

The Descendants of Shem Identified

Elam: Modern Poland

Asshur: Seventy years ago it was thought by some that Assyria descended from Abraham through Keturah. Since that time there has been an explosion of knowledge on ancient history and it is now understood that the Assyrians are actually descended from the Asshur son of Shem.

It was Asshur son of Shem who built Nineveh (Genesis 10:11) and founded the Assyrian peoples.

God later used the Assyrians to correct the Northern Ten Tribes of Israel c 721 B.C. and deport them from the Promised Land.

Remaining in the Promised Land was always CONDITIONAL on living by every Word of God.

> **Deuteronomy 30:15** See, I have set before thee this day life and good, and death and evil;
>
> **30:16** In that I command thee this day to love the LORD thy God, to walk in his ways, and to keep his commandments and his statutes and his judgments, that thou mayest live and multiply: and the LORD thy God shall bless thee in the land whither thou goest to possess it.
>
> **30:17** But if thine heart turn away, so that thou wilt not hear, but shalt be drawn away, and worship other gods, and serve them;
>
> **30:18** I denounce unto you this day, that ye shall surely perish, and that **ye shall not prolong your days upon the land,** whither thou passest over Jordan to go to possess it.
>
> **30:19** I call heaven and earth to record this day against you, that I have set before you life and death, blessing and cursing: therefore choose life, that both thou and thy seed may live:
>
> **30:20** That thou mayest love the LORD thy God, and that thou mayest obey his voice, and that thou mayest cleave unto him: for he is thy life, and the length of thy days: **that thou mayest dwell in the land** which the LORD sware unto thy fathers, to Abraham, to Isaac, and to Jacob, to give them.

Later the Assyrian Empire was supplanted by their brother people the Chaldeans, and the Assyrians migrated northwest taking the Ten Tribes of Israel with them.

A Partial Listing of Assyrian tribes:

Alemanni: Settled in Bavaria, Austria and Alsace

Boii: Settled in Bavaria

Quadi and Marcomani: settled in Bohemia and Moravia Czechoslovakia. At the close of WW 2 many went to Germany from the Sudetenland

Suabe: Settled in north Germany

Silesians: Settled in southwest Poland. After WW2 many migrated into Germany.

The Huns: were given Hungary [Hun-Land] by the Romans

The Ancient Assyrians today make up the modern nations of Germany, Austria and Hungary.

> **NOTE:** In the Middle Ages long after the Assyrians had migrated from the area, some Mesopotamian people were converted to the Eastern Orthodox Church.
>
> Although they had no connection with the Assyrian race, the Eastern Orthodox Church chose to call them Assyrian Christians based on their location in the heart of the ancient land of Assyria.
>
> Later some of them broke away to join Roman Catholicism and were called Chaldean Christians, again there is no racial connection to either the ancient Assyrians or Chaldeans

Lud: The Persians

Aram: 10:23 And **the children of Aram;** Uz, and Hul, and Gether, and Mash.

Aram: The Syrians

Arphaxad [Arpachshad]:

Father of the Chaldeans; Arpachshad was the progenitor of Ura and Kesed, who founded the city of *Ur Kesdim* (Ur of the Chaldees) on the west bank of the Euphrates

> **10:24** And **Arphaxad begat** Salah; and Salah begat Eber.
>
> **10:25** And **unto Eber were born two sons:** the name of one was Peleg; for in his days was the earth [the families were divided at Babel] divided;
>
> [The descendants of Peleg are listed in Genesis 11] and his [Peleg's] brother's name was Joktan.

The Family of Joktan were the Chaldeans and various peoples of Mesopotamia

> **10:26** And **Joktan begat** Almodad, and Sheleph, and Hazarmaveth, and Jerah,

10:27 And Hadoram, and Uzal, and Diklah,

10:28 And Obal, and Abimael, and Sheba,

10:29 And Ophir, and Havilah, and Jobab: all these were the sons of Joktan.

10:30 And their dwelling was from Mesha, as thou goest unto Sephar a mount of the east.

After the fall of the Chaldean Empire at Babylon, many Chaldean people migrated to southern Europe settling in the area we call southern Italy today.

10:31 These are the sons of Shem, after their families, after their tongues, in their lands, after their nations.

The Modern Palestinians

The Children of Joktan were the Chaldeans which included Abraham and Sarai. Other children of Joktan took up residence in Mesopotamia where they lived under the Assyrian Empire.

Because of the sins of Solomon, God took the Ten Tribes of Israel away splitting the Ten Tribes of Israel away from the Kingdom of Judah.

Then over many years as the Ten Tribes sinned and apostatized from God into idolatry and much wickedness, refusing to repent after many warnings; God withdrew his protection from the Ten Tribes.

The Assyrian Empire then attacked and in a series of successive waves overcame Israel in c 721 B.C. and carried them away from off the land.

2 Kings 17:6 In the ninth year of Hoshea the king of Assyria took Samaria, and carried Israel away into Assyria, and placed them in Halah and in Habor by the river of Gozan, and in the cities of the Medes.

17:7 For so it was, that the children of Israel had sinned against the LORD their God, which had brought them up out of the land of Egypt, from under the hand of Pharaoh king of Egypt, and had feared other gods, **17:8** And walked in the statutes of the heathen, whom the LORD cast out from before the children of Israel, and of the kings of Israel, which they had made.

The king of Assyria then brought in people from Mesopotamia to populate the land of Israel.

17:24 And the king of Assyria **brought men from Babylon, and from Cuthah, and from Ava, and from Hamath, and from Sepharvaim, and placed them in the cities of Samaria instead of the children of Israel:** and they possessed Samaria, and dwelt in the cities thereof.

Thus the area north of Jerusalem was populated by peoples from Mesopotamia. The capitol of the Ten Tribes was at Samaria and so the kingdom of the Ten Tribes of Israel was often called Samaria and these new migrants were afterwards called Samaritans.

Fast forwarding to the eighth century, Islam swept through the region and most of these folks converted to Islam, leaving only a few with the original Samaritan religion.

Today those few holding to the Samaritan religion are called Samaritans, but for political reasons the vast majority who are now Muslims are called Palestinians.

Ammon and Moab: Modern Jordan

After Abraham's nephew Lot had fled from the destruction of Sodom

Genesis 19:31 And the firstborn said unto the younger, Our father is old, and there is not a man in the earth to come in unto us after the manner of all the earth:

19:32 Come, let us make our father drink wine, and we will lie with him, that we may preserve seed of our father.

19:33 And they made their father drink wine that night: and the firstborn went in, and lay with her father; and he perceived not when she lay down, nor when she arose.

19:34 And it came to pass on the morrow, that the firstborn said unto the younger, Behold, I lay yesternight with my father: let us make him drink wine this night also; and go thou in, and lie with him, that we may preserve seed of our father.

19:35 And they made their father drink wine that night also: and the younger arose, and lay with him; and he perceived not when she lay down, nor when she arose.

19:36 Thus were both the daughters of Lot with child by their father.

19:37 And the first born bare a son, and called his name Moab: the same is the father of **the Moabites unto this day.**

19:38 And the younger, she also bare a son, and called his name Benammi: the same is the father of **the children of Ammon unto this day**.

The Arab Peoples

Genesis 11:30 But Sarai was barren; she had no child.

Abram and Sarai had longed for a child all of their lives and now that Sarai was old and well past child bearing, she sought a child by giving her maid to her husband.

In due time Hagar gave birth to a son Ishmael and began to despise Sarai and Sarai treated her very badly, but God gave Hagar a blessing for Ishmael.

> **Genesis 16:10** And the angel of the LORD said unto her, I will multiply thy seed exceedingly, that it shall not be numbered for multitude.
>
> **16:11** And the angel of the LORD said unto her, Behold, thou art with child and shalt bear a son, and shalt call his name Ishmael; because the LORD hath heard thy affliction.

16:12 And he will be a wild man; his hand will be against every man, and every man's hand against him; and he shall dwell in the presence of all his brethren [near to Israel].

Then God gave a child by his promise to Sarai.

Then filled with jealousy Sarai drove Hagar and Ishmael out.

Genesis 21:10 Wherefore she said unto Abraham, Cast out this bondwoman and her son: for the son of this bondwoman shall not be heir with my son, even with Isaac.

21:11 And the thing was very grievous in Abraham's sight because of his son.

21:12 And God said unto Abraham, Let it not be grievous in thy sight because of the lad, and because of thy bondwoman; in all that Sarah hath said unto thee, hearken unto her voice; for in Isaac shall thy seed be called.

21:13 And **also of the son of the bondwoman will I make a nation, because he is thy seed.**

21:14 And Abraham rose up early in the morning, and took bread, and a bottle of water, and gave it unto Hagar, putting it on her shoulder, and the child, and sent her away: and she departed, and wandered in the wilderness of Beersheba.

21:15 And the water was spent in the bottle, and she cast the child under one of the shrubs.

21:16 And she went, and sat her down over against him a good way off, as it were a bow shot: for she said, Let me not see the death of the child. And she sat over against him, and lift up her voice, and wept.

21:17 And God heard the voice of the lad; and the angel of God called to Hagar out of heaven, and said unto her, What aileth thee, Hagar? fear not; for God hath heard the voice of the lad where he is.

21:18 Arise, lift up the lad, and hold him in thine hand; for **I will make him a great nation.**

21:19 And God opened her eyes, and she saw a well of water; and she went, and filled the bottle with water, and gave the lad drink.

The Hagarenes

The Hagarenes are not of the family of Abraham, but being the children of Hagar by another later husband are mentioned here.

After Hagar was driven out with Ishmael the son of Abraham, she remarried and had other sons. These other sons are called Hagarines to differentiate them from Ishmael the son of Abraham.

These descendants of Hagar dwelt with the descendants of Ishmael. The various sons of Hagar including Ishmael are the Arab peoples living today in the countries on the Arabian Peninsula.

Esau

Esau can be found in scripture under the names Esau, Edom, Mount Seir, Temen [the word Turkmen comes from Temen] and the various tribes of Esau notably the Amalekites.

> **Genesis 25:30** And Esau said to Jacob, Feed me, I pray thee, with that same red pottage; for I am faint: therefore was his name called **Edom**.

> **Genesis 36:8** Thus dwelt Esau in **mount Seir: Esau is Edom.**

Esau and Jacob were twin brothers. The story begins in:

> **Genesis 25:21** And Isaac intreated the LORD for his wife, because she was barren: and the LORD was intreated of him, and Rebekah his wife conceived.

> **25:22** And the children struggled together within her; and she said, If it be so, why am I thus? And she went to enquire of the LORD.

25:23 And the LORD said unto her, Two nations are in thy womb, and two manner of people shall be separated from thy bowels; and the one people shall be stronger than the other people; and the elder shall serve the younger.

25:24 And when her days to be delivered were fulfilled, behold, there were twins in her womb.

As the story continues Jacob takes advantage of Esau and buys from him a priceless birthright for a bowl of stew. This is an important lesson for us that we should value the birthright of eternal life very highly and not sell it for the temporary pleasures of the flesh.

Later Jacob steals the blessing reserved for the first born Esau by a deception, forcing him to flee for his life from an enraged Esau.

Then after many years in exile Jacob returns home to make peace with his brother. This part of the story ends as Esau chooses to live in Mount Seir and Jacob in Shechem.

Genesis 33:16 So Esau returned that day on his way unto Seir

33:17 And Jacob journeyed to Succoth, and built him an house, and made booths for his cattle: therefore the name of the place is called Succoth.

After Israel came out from Egypt, over the ensuing centuries Edom was overrun by Egypt, Babylon, Arabs, and Jordanians, and the people of Edom [Esau] migrated away from that place.

Esau migrated to central Asia where they founded the nation of Turkmenistan. Later in the eighth century A.D. Islam spread rapidly and certain of the tribes of Turkmens [from Temen; Esau], notably the Othmani and Amalekites joined in spreading the faith by war conquering the area now called Turkey and founding the Ottoman [Othmani] Empire.

Today the tribes of Esau are divided between the people of central Asia called Turkmens and the modern nation of Turkey.

Genesis 36:9 And these are the generations of Esau the father of the Edomites in mount Seir:

36:10 These are the names of Esau's sons; **Eliphaz** the son of Adah the wife of Esau, **Reuel** the son of Bashemath the wife of Esau.

36:11 And **the sons of Eliphaz** were **Teman**, Omar, Zepho, and Gatam, and Kenaz.

36:12 And Timna was concubine to Eliphaz Esau's son; and she bare to Eliphaz **Amalek** [the Amalekites]: these were the sons of Adah Esau's wife.

Mount Seir was named for Seir, the Horite, whose offspring had inhabited the area (Genesis 14:6, 36:20) until the children of Esau (the Edomites) completely destroyed the Horites and took possession of the city (Deuteronomy 2:4-5, 12, 22).

From that time Seir has become synonymous with Esau who took possession of Seir and destroyed the Horites living there. (Genesis 32:3; 33:14, 16; 36:8; Joshua 24:4).

The main cities of Esau [Edom] were Seir and Petra until they were removed to the north into the area now called the Stan countries, particularly Turkmenistan. After they accepted Islam in the eighth century many of the Turkic tribes including the Othmani and Amalekites, swept into Turkey and established the Othmani [Ottoman] Empire.

The Ottoman Empire collapsed at the end of WW 1 and today Turkey is struggling with Egypt to gain back leadership of the Muslim world.

Today the tribes of Esau are divided between Turkmenistan in Central Asia and Turkey.

Appendix 2

The Family of Abraham

See also: Assyria

Genesis 11:18 And Peleg lived thirty years, and begat **Reu**:

11:19 And Peleg lived after he begat Reu two hundred and nine years, and begat sons and daughters.

11:20 And Reu lived two and thirty years, and begat **Serug**:

11:21 And Reu lived after he begat Serug two hundred and seven years, and begat sons and daughters.

11:22 And Serug lived thirty years, and begat **Nahor**:

11:23 And Serug lived after he begat Nahor two hundred years, and begat sons and daughters.

11:24 And Nahor lived nine and twenty years, and begat **Terah**:

11:25 And Nahor lived after he begat Terah an hundred and nineteen years, and begat sons and daughters.

11:26 And Terah lived seventy years, and begat **Abram, Nahor, and Haran.**

11:27 Now these are the generations of Terah: Terah begat Abram, Nahor, and Haran; and **Haran begat Lot.**

11:28 And Haran died before his father Terah in the land of his nativity, in Ur of the Chaldees.

Abram was the father of Isaac who fathered Jacob.

In Genesis we are told that Jacob was renamed Israel by God.

> **Genesis 32:28** And he said, Thy name shall be called no more Jacob, but **Israel**: for as a prince hast thou power with God and with men, and hast prevailed.

Jacob persevered and prevailed.

Later we learn that Israel [Jacob] had twelve sons, and each was to grow to become a tribe. Then when they were in Egypt God gave a double portion, which is the right of the first born, to Joseph and his two sons Ephraim and Manasseh making each a full tribe in Israel; and Levi was called out of Israel to become the tribe of God, or the priesthood tribe.

When Israel entered the Promised Land the nation consisted of one priesthood tribe and twelve tribes each with its own area, only one of which was Judah or the Jews.

Then during the days of Solomon because of his sins in exalting idols God, told Solomon that he would break the bounds of brotherhood between the ten tribes of Israel and Judah, removing the northern ten tribes of Israel from the kingdom.

> **1 Kings 11:9** And the LORD was angry with Solomon, because his heart was turned from the LORD God of Israel, which had appeared unto him twice,
>
> **11:10** And had commanded him concerning this thing, that he should not go after other gods: but he kept not that which the LORD commanded.

11:11 Wherefore the LORD said unto Solomon, Forasmuch as this is done of thee, and thou hast not kept my covenant and my statutes, which I have commanded thee, I will surely rend the kingdom from thee, and will give it to thy servant.

11:12 Notwithstanding in thy days I will not do it for David thy father's sake: but I will rend it out of the hand of thy son.

11:13 Howbeit I will not rend away all the kingdom; but will give one tribe to thy son for David my servant's sake, and for Jerusalem's sake which I have chosen.

Then after Solomon had died, God rent the ten tribes of Israel from the kingdom of Judah in this manner:

1 Kings 12:3 That they sent and called him. And Jeroboam and all the congregation of Israel came, and spake unto Rehoboam, saying,

12:4 Thy father made our yoke grievous: now therefore make thou the grievous service of thy father, and his heavy yoke which he put upon us, lighter, and we will serve thee.

12:5 And he said unto them, Depart yet for three days, then come again to me. And the people departed.

12:6 And king Rehoboam consulted with the old men, that stood before Solomon his father while he yet lived, and said, How do ye advise that I may answer this people?

12:7 And they spake unto him, saying, If thou wilt be a servant unto this people this day, and wilt serve them, and answer them, and speak good words to them, then they will be thy servants for ever.

12:8 But he forsook the counsel of the old men, which they had given him, and consulted with the young men that were grown up with him, and which stood before him: **12:9** And he said unto them, What counsel give ye that we may answer this people, who have spoken to me, saying, Make the yoke which thy father did put upon us lighter?

12:10 And the young men that were grown up with him spake unto him, saying, Thus shalt thou speak unto this people that spake unto thee, saying, Thy father made our yoke heavy, but make thou it lighter unto us; thus shalt thou say unto them, My little finger shall be thicker than my father's loins.

12:11 And now whereas my father did lade you with a heavy yoke, I will add to your yoke: my father hath chastised you with whips, but I will chastise you with scorpions.

12:12 So Jeroboam and all the people came to Rehoboam the third day, as the king had appointed, saying, Come to me again the third day.

12:13 And the king answered the people roughly, and forsook the old men's counsel that they gave him; **12:14** And spake to them after the counsel of the young men, saying, My father made your yoke heavy, and I will add to your yoke: my father also chastised you with whips, but I will chastise you with scorpions [many tailed whips].

12:15 Wherefore the king hearkened not unto the people; for the cause was from the LORD, that he might perform his saying, which the LORD spake by Ahijah the Shilonite unto Jeroboam the son of Nebat.

12:16 So when all Israel saw that the king hearkened not unto them, the people answered the king, saying, What portion have we in David? neither have we inheritance in the son of Jesse: to your tents, O Israel: now see to thine own house, David. So Israel departed unto their tents.

Then the ten tribes of Israel were separated from the Tribe of Judah; the tribe of Benjamin remaining with Judah, because their land bordered on Judah and surrounded Jerusalem. The priestly tribe of Levi which belonged to God also remained at Jerusalem.

From here the Bible is full of the rivalries and wars between Judah and Israel, and records the sins of both the Kingdom of Israel and the Kingdom of Judah.

The Kingdom of Israel immediately began to fall into idolatry as Jeroboam set up idols in the land for fear that Israel would rebel against him when they went up to Jerusalem to keep the annual Festivals of God.

1 Kings 12:26 And Jeroboam said in his heart, Now shall the kingdom return to the house of David:

12:27 If this people go up to do sacrifice in the house of the LORD at Jerusalem, then shall the heart of this people turn again unto their lord, even unto Rehoboam king of Judah, and they shall kill me, and go again to Rehoboam king of Judah.

12:28 Whereupon the king took counsel, and made two calves of gold, and said unto them, It is too much for you to go up to Jerusalem: behold thy gods, O Israel, which brought thee up out of the land of Egypt.

12:29 And he set the one in Bethel, and the other put he in Dan. **12:30** And this thing became a sin: for the people went to worship before the one, even unto Dan.

12:31 And he made an house of high places, and made priests of the lowest of the people, which were not of the sons of Levi.

12:32 And Jeroboam ordained a feast in the eighth month, on the fifteenth day of the month, like unto the feast that is in Judah, and he offered upon the altar. So did he in Bethel, sacrificing unto the calves that he had made: and he placed in Bethel the priests of the high places which he had made.

From that time onward God repeatedly sent his prophets over many years to warn Israel to repent until finally God removed his blessings and allowed waves of Assyrians to sweep into Israel, finally culminating in the fall of the capitol Samaria   c721 B.C. and the removal of the ten tribes.

Some in Israel repented at the preaching of the prophets and especially when Judah had good kings, some did migrate to Judea where they were assimilated into Judah, but the nation as a whole did not turn from their wicked ways.

2 Kings 17:6 In the ninth year of Hoshea the king of Assyria took Samaria, and carried Israel away into Assyria, and placed them in Halah and in Habor by the river of Gozan, and in the cities of the Medes.

17:7 For so it was, that the children of Israel had sinned against the LORD their God, which had brought them up out of the land of Egypt, from under the hand of Pharaoh king of Egypt, and had feared other gods,

17:8 And walked in the statutes of the heathen, whom the LORD cast out from before the children of Israel, and of the kings of Israel, which they had made.

These ten tribes of Israel then migrated with the Assyrians into North-Western Europe.

Modern Locations of the Twelve Tribes of Israel

To understand where they migrated to and where the so called "lost" ten tribes may be found today, it is important to see what Bible prophecy says about the tribes of Israel for the latter days and then to look at the history and migrations of these nations.

The Bible prophecies that most of the tribes of Israel would be independent nations and several would become more than one latter day nation.

These prophecies are only partially fulfilled at this time due to the sins of the nations. They will be realized in their fullness in the millennial Kingdom of God.

At that time the tribes of Israel will continue and prosper in their various prophesied locations while a core population of each tribe of Israel will be brought back to the physical Promised Land and the division between Israel and Judah will be healed

Deuteronomy 33

Moses before his death blessed the tribes and prophesied from God about their latter days when they shall become many independent nations on this earth

> **Deuteronomy 33:1** And **this is the blessing, wherewith Moses the man of God blessed the children of Israel before his death.**
>
> **33:2** And he said, The LORD came from Sinai, and rose up from Seir unto them; he shined forth from mount Paran, and he came with ten thousands of saints: from his right hand went a fiery law for them.
>
> **33:3** Yea, he loved the people; all his saints are in thy hand: and they sat down at thy feet; every one shall receive of thy words.
>
> **33:4** Moses commanded us a law, even the inheritance of the congregation of Jacob [Israel].
>
> **33:5** And he [God] was king in **Jeshurun**, when the heads of the people and the tribes of Israel were gathered together.

Jeshurun (Hebrew: יְשֻׁרוּן), in the Hebrew Bible, is a poetic name for Israel, derived from a root word meaning upright, just or straight. Jeshurun appears four times in the Hebrew Bible — three times in Deuteronomy and once in Isaiah. It can mean the people of Israel (Deut. 32:15; 33:26), the Land of Israel (Deut. 33:5;), or the Patriarch Jacob (whom an Angel renamed Israel in Genesis 32:29):

From this point I am going to add the Prophetic Blessings of Jacob in Gen 49, to the Prophetic Blessings of Moses for a fuller picture of each tribe in the latter days.

Reuben

Deuteronomy 33:6 Let Reuben live, and not die; and let not his men be few.

> **Genesis 49:3** Reuben, thou art my firstborn, my might, and the beginning of my strength, the excellency of dignity, and the excellency of power: ⁴Unstable as water, thou shalt not excel; because thou wentest up to thy father's bed; then defiledst thou it: he went up to my couch.

Reuben is not to become an independent nation in his own right in the latter days because of instability.

The tribe of Reuben became a part of the people migrating with the Germanic tribes of Assyria after the fall of the Assyrian Empire. Known as Normans [North Men] **Reuben settled in Normandy in northern France.**

There is absolutely no doubt that Reuben migrated into northern France, but to say that they dominate and control France today defies the prophecy for Reuben.

Even to say that Reuben remained in France in large numbers is a mere supposition since so many hundreds of thousands of people migrated to the new world from France in the 17 and 1800's.

Later most of them migrated to Canada and became the Quebecois, others migrated to New Orleans from Normandy, and some were expelled from Eastern Canada by the British ending up in the US where they are called Cajuns and Acadians.

The term Norman means North Men and is a general term for those tribes of Israel who migrated north into Scandinavia; some of them remaining in Scandinavia and others sweeping out into Britain and Normandy

Normandy takes its name from the invaders from the north collectively called Vikings or North Men; who menaced large parts of Europe towards the end of the 1st millennium in two phases (790–930, then 980–1030). Medieval Latin documents referred to them as Normanni, which means "men of the North". This name provides the etymological basis for the modern words "Norman" and "Normandy",

Most French Canadians originate from Normandy and they came from what is now called Upper Normandy, Lower Normandy and the Channel Islands.

For the nation of modern France See: The Hittites

Judah

Deuteronomy 33:7 And this is the blessing of Judah: and he said, Hear, LORD, the voice of Judah, and bring him unto his people: let his hands be sufficient for him; and be thou an help to him from his enemies.

> **Genesis 49:8** Judah, thou art he whom thy brethren shall praise: thy hand shall be in the neck of thine enemies; thy father's children shall bow down before thee. **49:9** Judah is a lion's whelp: from the prey, my son, thou art gone up: he stooped down, he couched as a lion, and as an old lion; who shall rouse him up?
>
> **49:10** The sceptre shall not depart from Judah, nor a lawgiver from between his feet, until Shiloh [Christ] come; and unto him shall the gathering of the people be. **49:11** Binding his foal unto the vine, and his ass's colt unto the choice vine; he washed his garments in wine, and his clothes in the blood of grapes: **49:12** His eyes shall be red with wine, and his teeth white with milk.

Judah is to be blessed with leadership skills and be a self sufficient people and will ultimately be respected by the nations. Messiah the Christ shall come to Judah at Jerusalem first.

Today the Jews are scattered worldwide but about half of them occupy the present Jewish State

Levi

Levi was chosen to be the priests of God, yet many of them would strive with God and did rebel against God.

Deuteronomy 33:8 And of Levi he said, Let thy Thummim and thy Urim be with thy holy one, whom thou didst prove at Massah, and with whom thou didst strive at the waters of Meribah;

Yet many [the sons of Zadok] shall serve in the millennial temple; because of the godly loyalty of their father Zadok.

> **Ezekiel 44:15** But the priests the Levites, the sons of **Zadok**, that kept the charge of my sanctuary when the children of Israel went astray from me, they shall come near to me to minister unto me, and they shall stand before me to offer unto me the fat and the blood, saith the Lord God:

Deuteronomy 33:9 Who said unto his father and to his mother, I have not seen him; neither did he acknowledge his brethren, nor knew his own children: for **they have observed thy word, and kept thy covenant.**

In the millennium Levi via the descendants of Zadok shall yet serve God to teach the people righteousness.

33:10 They **shall teach Jacob thy judgments, and Israel thy law:** they shall put incense [representing the prayers of the faithful] before thee, and whole burnt sacrifice [representing wholehearted service to God] upon thine altar.

A blessing for the faithful of Levi during the millennium

They shall prosper serving God in his millennial Temple and no enemy shall touch them.

33:11 Bless, LORD, his substance, and accept the work of his hands; smite through the loins of them that rise against him, and of them that hate him, that they rise not again.

When the northern Ten Tribes of Israel were separated from Judah; Levi remained at the temple in Jerusalem and is largely scattered among the Jews today.

Simeon

Levi and Simeon were men of temper not to become independent nations and are to be divided [scattered] in Israel

> **Genesis 49:5** Simeon and Levi are brethren; instruments of cruelty are in their habitations. **49:6** O my soul, come not thou into their secret; unto their assembly, mine honour, be not thou united: for in their anger they slew a man, and in their selfwill they digged down a wall. **49:7** Cursed be their anger, for it was fierce; and their wrath, for it was cruel: I will divide them in Jacob, and scatter them in Israel.

Today Levi is scattered mainly in Judah, while Simeon is the Simonii [Welsh] living in Wales and possibly the Scotts.

Benjamin would be a strong people which would dwell together with Judah.

Deuteronomy 33:12 And of Benjamin he said, **The beloved of the LORD** [Judah] **shall dwell in safety by him** [Benjamin and Judah will dwell together]; and the Lord shall cover [defend] him all the day long, and he shall dwell between his shoulders.

> **Genesis 49:27** Benjamin shall ravin as a wolf: in the morning he shall devour the prey, and at night he shall divide the spoil

When the Ten Tribes were separated from Judah Benjamin remained with Judah 1 Kings 12:21, 1 Chronicles 11:1 and 2 Chronicles 34:9.

Joseph

Ephraim (The British Peoples) and Manasseh (the founding Anglo Saxon American peoples)

Joseph replaced Reuben as the first born and was granted a double portion to become many nations.

Deuteronomy 33:13 And of Joseph he said, Blessed of the LORD be his land, for the precious things of heaven, for the dew, and for the deep that coucheth beneath,

33:14 And for the precious fruits brought forth by the sun, and for the precious things put forth by the moon,

33:15 And for the chief things of the ancient mountains, and for the precious things of the lasting hills,

33:16 And for the precious things of the earth and fulness thereof, and for the good will of him that dwelt in the bush: let the blessing come upon the head of Joseph, and upon the top of the head of him that was separated from his brethren.

The question has come up: Why is Ephraim ascribed ten thousands and Manasseh only thousands when America has a much larger population than the British peoples?

The answer is a translation issue

In Deuteronomy 33:17 thousands and ten thousands are mistranslation

The term "thousands" used for Manasseh actually means an innumerable multitude.

http://biblehub.com/greek/4519.htm

The term "ten thousands" for Ephraim, more properly means a myriad or large number.

http://lexiconcordance.com/hebrew/7233.html

The translator from 1611 simply made an error. Deu 33:17 properly reads.

> **Deuteronomy 33:17** His [Joseph's; BOTH Ephraim and Manasseh] glory is like the firstling of his bullock, and his horns are like the horns of unicorns: with them he shall push the people together to the ends of the earth: and they are the ten thousands [properly: multitudes] of Ephraim, and they are the thousands [properly: innumerable multitudes] of Manasseh.

[The Anglo Saxon British and Americans] shall be warlike and fight many wars, and shall have mighty blessing of good things.

> **Genesis 49:22** Joseph is a fruitful bough, even a fruitful bough by a well; whose branches run over the wall: **49:23** [They will have many enemies and much war, but will be blessed by God with great strength over their enemies] The archers have sorely grieved him, and shot at him, and hated him: **49:24** But his bow abode in strength, and the arms of his hands were **made strong by the hands of the mighty God of Jacob;**
>
> **49:25** Even by the God of thy father [Abraham], who shall help thee; and by the Almighty, who shall bless thee with blessings of heaven above, blessings of the deep that lieth under, blessings of the breasts, and of the womb:
>
> **49:26** The blessings of thy father have prevailed above the blessings of my progenitors unto the utmost bound of the everlasting hills: they shall be on the head of Joseph, and on the crown of the head of him that was separate from his brethren.

Zebulun

Zebulun is to dwell by the sea and be a port for ships, like unto the port of Zidon.

Deuteronomy 33:18 And of Zebulun he said, Rejoice, Zebulun, in thy going out; and, Issachar, in thy tents.

33:19 They shall call the people unto the mountain [In the millennium they shall turn to God and call the nations to go up to the mountain of the Lord]; there they shall offer sacrifices of righteousness: for they shall suck of the abundance of the seas, and of treasures hid in the sand.

Genesis 49:13 Zebulun shall dwell at the haven of the sea; and he shall be for an haven of ships; and his border [the greatness of his port shall be like Zidon] shall be unto [like] Zidon.

The tribe of Zebulun are the [Frisians-Daci-Belgae] today called the Netherlands or Dutch people and their great ports are Amsterdam and Rotterdam.

Issachar

Genesis 49:14 Issachar is a strong ass couching down between two burdens: **15** And he saw that rest was good, and the land that it was pleasant; and bowed his shoulder to bear, and became a servant unto tribute.

Issachar is the Suomi, Finland; the official name of Finland is Suomi Finland

Gad

Deuteronomy 33:20 And of Gad he said, Blessed be he that enlargeth Gad: he dwelleth as a lion, and teareth the arm with the crown of the head.

33:21 And he provided the first part for himself, because there, in a portion of the lawgiver, was he seated; and he came with the heads of the people, he executed the justice of the LORD, and his judgments with Israel.

> **Genesis 49:19** Gad, a troop shall overcome him: but he shall overcome at the last.

Gad shall be overcome but will overcome in the end, and in the millennium is to be a respected diplomatic and legal nation enforcing godly justice.

Dan

Deuteronomy 33:22 And of Dan he said, Dan is a lion's whelp: he shall leap from Bashan.

> **Genesis 49:16** Dan shall judge his people, as one of the tribes of Israel. Dan shall be a serpent by the way, an adder in the path, that biteth the horse heels, so that his rider shall fall backward.

Dan shall leap from Bashan [the North], he shall have his own nation and shall vex his brothers. This speaking of the Irish [Dan] fight with the British [Ephraim].

The Patriarch Dan was born from the handmaid of Rachel, Bilhah. Rachel was in envy of her sister Leah. She wanted so badly to bear a child for Jacob, that she gave him her handmaid to bear a son. That son was Dan. When he was born she said, "God hath judged me, and hath also heard my voice, and hath given me a son: therefore called she his name Dan." (Gen 30:6). he meaning of the word "Dan" is "Judge" (Strong's #1777 "judge").

When Israel took possession of the promised land, the tribe of Dan was allotted its tribal inheritance in the South Western area of that land.. Dan was situated west-Northwest of Judah; Dan's territory was on the Mediterranean Sea, and included the busy port of Joppa, next to modern Tel-Aviv (Joshua 19:40-48).

Many Danes later left the land sailing from Joppa in ships while others migrated northwards to Laish, and called the city Dan, after their father, see Judges 18.

The northern city Laish, renamed Dan, by the tribe of Dan, was about thirty miles inland from the ancient busy port of Tyre.

Dan was divided into two halves as an early migration by ship to Ireland was later followed by a second migration with their Assyrian [Germanic] captors from Laish [Dan] ending up in Denmark.

The western Irish half tribe has vexed Ephraim, while the eastern Danish half tribe has been a peaceable nation.

Naphtali

Naphtali is to be known for wise words.

Deuteronomy 33:23 And of Naphtali he said, O Naphtali, satisfied with favour, and full with the blessing of the LORD: possess thou the west and the south [properly the sea or a long sea coast (such as Sweden) Strong's H3220].

> **Genesis 49:21** Naphtali is a hind let loose [a swift and agile warrior]: he giveth goodly words.

Naphtali the Sved-Daci-Ephtalites – Naphtalites; Norway, Sweden

Asher

Asher shall be strong all his days, be wealthy and have access to oil.

Deuteronomy 33:24 And of Asher he said, Let Asher be blessed with children; let him be acceptable to his brethren, and let him dip his foot in oil.

33:25 Thy shoes shall be iron and brass; and as thy days, so shall thy strength be.

> **Genesis 49:20** Out of Asher his bread shall be fat, and he shall yield royal dainties.

All Israel and their nations shall be blessed of the Eternal in the Kingdom of God.

Brethren, these prophecies are only in part for now, and are to be fulfilled in the Kingdom of God when all Israel repents and turns to the Eternal with a whole heart.

Jeshurun (Hebrew: יְשֻׁרוּן), in the Hebrew Bible, is a poetic name for Israel, derived from a root word meaning upright, just or straight. Jeshurun appears four times in the Hebrew Bible — three times in Deuteronomy and once in Isaiah. It can mean the people of Israel (Deut. 32:15; 33:26), the Land of Israel (Deut. 33:5;), or the Patriarch Jacob (whom an Angel renamed Israel in Genesis 32:29):

Deuteronomy 33:26 There is none like unto the God of Jeshurun, who rideth upon the heaven in thy help, and in his excellency on the sky.

33:27 The eternal God is thy refuge, and underneath are the everlasting arms: and he shall thrust out the enemy from before thee; and shall say, Destroy them.

33:28 Israel then shall dwell in safety alone: the fountain of Jacob shall be upon a land of corn and wine; also his heavens shall drop down dew.

33:29 Happy art thou, O Israel: who is like unto thee, O people saved by the LORD, the shield of thy help, and who is the sword of thy excellency! and thine enemies shall be found liars unto thee; and thou shalt tread upon their high places.

.

Possession of the Promised Land

When Israel was about to enter the Promised Land Moses wrote his fifth book called Deuteronomy.

In that book Moses recounted the history of Israel from their departure out of Egypt and warned the people from God that their possession of the Land was absolutely CONDITIONAL on them faithfully living by EVERY WORD of God.

> **Deuteronomy 4:1** Now therefore **hearken, O Israel, unto the statutes and unto the judgments, which I teach you, for to do them, that ye may live, and go in and possess the land which the LORD God of your fathers giveth you.**
>
> **4:2** Ye shall not add unto the word which I command you, neither shall ye diminish ought from it, that ye may keep the commandments of the LORD your God which I command you.

4:3 Your eyes have seen what the LORD did because of Baalpeor: for all the men that followed Baalpeor, **the LORD thy God hath destroyed them from among you.**

The history of Israel from the time they left Egypt until this day is that God cares for those who faithfully follow him to live by His Word; and God will strongly rebuke those who depart from the Word of God to do as they please and follow anyone other than God and God's Word; which is the sin of idolatry.

Historically God removed the Ten Tribes of Israel from off their land when they would not stop their wickedness and idolatries.

Later Judah was also removed from the land by God through the hand of the Babylonians and again then by the Romans for their pride and sins. If we are full of sin today, God will again correct us! For Almighty God is consistent.

Look at Judah in Palestine today and you will find a secular state where 80% of the Jews are not religious; and the 20% who are religious follow their own traditions. It is the same in Britain and America who profess godliness as we fill our lands with wickedness.

Today Britain, America and the Jewish State are overspread with wickedness against the Word of God and we close our eyes to what God did to our forefathers for these same sins and think that they can continue to be blessed and remain on the land without any correction from God.

The other nations of the Ten Tribes of Israel are no better. We have been given the fairest portions of the earth and have been blessed above all people in all of history, being given riches unimaginable to people of a few centuries ago and these blessings have filled us with pride and the false assumption that we are a righteous people as we fill our lands with the sins of our forefathers.

It is beyond any argument that today's British peoples, America, the Dutch, Scandinavia and the Jewish state are full of Sabbath breaking, cheating, corruption and stealing; lying, adultery, fornication and homosexuality, followers of the occult and overwhelming idolatry [placing things between us and God].

Yes all of the other nations on earth are just as bad, but we are the ones who have received God's blessings; we are the ones who are supposed to be an example of righteousness for the earth.

We have utterly failed so God will withdraw his blessings and his protection that we might be an example of what happens when men defy God. Without God's blessings we shall surely fall, after which the turn of the other nations will come; until all humanity is humbled and ready to accept the coming of Messiah the Christ to save us and to rule all nations in godly righteousness.

Visit Our Website

theshininglight.info